To:Duane: 6-28-2018

ROLLER COASTER

VICTOR S. GREWAL

Thank you for your
support! ZERO DUI's
My only hope!

Vick

Some names and identifying details have been changed to protect the privacy of individuals

ISBN: 978-0692765197

A portion of every sale from this book will go to the Kalvi Institute for the brain and mind at University California San Diego, toward finding a cure for paralysis and for those who have sustained brain injuries.

Table of Contents

Dedications

This book would not be possible if it was not for the many people who encouraged and reminded me of how important my story is. Nearly everyone, after hearing my story, tells me to write a book, to share it, reminding me that everybody has a purpose in this world. My purpose is to share this very tragic story and how I found my strength to persevere thanks to my faith in Jesus Christ.

To my loving parents, who taught me right from wrong, they raised my brother and I in difficult times. I thank God for both of you every day. You gave me a strong faith in God Almighty and when times were rough, both told me to NEVER give up, reminding me God is in control and he will take care of everything!

To those who drink, do drugs and then drive, I hope my story is a vivid reminder that this behavior is never a wise choice. A big reason I am writing this book is to end this nonsense.

Nearly every evening, when I watch the evening news, I hear the same story over and over:

"Person hit by a drunk driver."

"A person with a third DUI offense injures a young girl who had come home from the University of Florida to visit her parents."

"3:00 a.m., a woman who was drunk three times over the legal limit crashed car into a coffee shop."

I hear these stories all too often and it breaks my heart.

To all who have allowed me to touch other lives, I want to thank you for the opportunities that you have given me to share my story. To The Fox 5 News team and Leslie Markus, thank you so much for allowing me to share my story with your many viewers. To Mothers Against Drunk Driving (MADD) thank you, Paula Myers, for allowing me to urge DUI offenders to not drink and drive ever again.

Ian MacGregor, thank you for allowing me to talk at The Annual Teen Driving Safety event you and your team organized. Thank you for believing in me and trusting me to empower other people to never drink and drive. To the San Dieguito Drug Alliance team, thank you. I am not a public speaker and never intended to be, but if by sharing my story helps to reduce the number of DUI's, injuries, or deaths caused by drunk drivers, then it is all worth it.

Thank you to Joe Olesky, the teacher who allowed me to come to his REDI program class at San Dieguito Acadamy, and for allowing me to relate my story with your students.

Thank you Pastor Jason Graves at Daybreak Church for helping to solidify my faith in Jesus along with the wonderful staff there. Prayers do come true and for that reason, I would like to thank the amazing prayer team. Thank you Jesus for guiding me to such a wonderful church.

Mandy S. Gish, thank you for all the love and friendship you have brought into my life since 1987. We were only young kids back then but now are mature adults ready to take on the world. You helped me to put a smile on my face when life took a downhill dive, and celebrated with me on all of the pleasant times in life. Thank you for all the time that you devoted with me to proofread this story.

Last but not least I would like to make a huge shout out and dedication to my good friend and brother in Christ Ulises Hernadez Guzman, who I met at The Nursing Home a few years ago. God has a way of bringing friends together and I am glad our friendship began in a totally unexpected way. Thank you for the magic of our friendship!

Most importantly, thank you Jesus for helping me, guiding me and for being my strength in life. Without you, nothing is possible.

DEDICATION PICTURES! SO YOU KNOW ALL THE AWESOME PEOPLE WHO HAVE HELPED ME!

Went on Fox 5 news twice in one year sharing my story with the many viewers.

Ulises Hernandez Guzman

Jesus Christ- My LORD and Savior!

My mom and dad!

Fox 5 former producer Leslie Marcus

Mandy Gish and I posing for a photo with our elementary school principal who we bumped into at Barnes and Nobles

Mandy Gish and I posing for a photo
with our elementary school principal
who we bumped into at Barnes and
Nobles

Arshdeep Brar: Birthday January 4, 2012
Killed by a drunk driver three days after
his 20th birthday.

Prologue

"Help somebody...anybody...please help me," I said waking up from a two month coma.

What happened... where am I..."?

"Hello, my son," said a voice from the other side of the room.

As my head slowly moved away from the left light beige wall to the right side of the room I saw my dad in a hospital bed with a brace around his neck. He was looking straight up at the ceiling.

"Dad what are you doing over there and what am I doing over here? Help me dad. I feel cold and I need another blanket. It is cold in this room. Come and help me dad."

"I cannot help you as now I cannot even help myself," his voice started to crack.

"Let me call the nurse," my dad said.

"Dad what is this needle doing in my left arm for? What is that beeping noise? Where am I

dad? I am scared."

"Yes, may I help you?" said Kathleen, the evening Licensed Vocational Nurse, as she entered.

"Can you please get another blanket for my son and straighten the pillow under my neck? It doesn't feel very comfortable."

As Kathleen was putting the blanket over me, I asked where I was and how did I get here? Her silence spoke volumes.

"Please don't tell him anything. I will tell him. I don't want him to get more scared than he already is."

"Your daddy will tell you dear. I just want you to know that I will try to help you as much as I can. Please feel free to call me. Push this button above your head for assistance."

After she left, my dad and I sat in the room with the TV off. For five minutes the only sound was the beeping of the heart monitor.

"Oh dad please tell me how I got here! I am scared," I pleaded.

"One evening, after all of us were all tired from the day's activities, all of us wanted to go out for a drive. We went to K-Mart to buy some things for the house. A drive I wish we would have not taken..."

As I listened patiently I was waiting for the answer to my question. "Go on Dad... please tell me."

"As I was driving the car and we were all enjoying our family time after shopping, a person who was drunk and on drugs failed to stop at the stop sign, crashing into our car. We were all injured but the ones who received the biggest injuries were you and I."

I started to tremble with fear... I noticed how the left side of my body could not move.

"Oh dad what happened to me? The left side of my body cannot move!"

"You were left with a traumatic brain injury and that is why the left side of your body is unable to move. I'm sorry son. There is good news though my son."

"Good news... How can there be any good news in all of this mess?" I asked myself.

"The good news is that your mother and brother did not get severe injuries or get very badly hurt. They will be here soon."

"What about us dad? When will I be able to use the left side of my body? When will you be able to walk again dad so you and I can walk out of this room and go play in the park?"

It seemed like a bad dream, with no way out. My 5-year-old mind imagined my dad and I out in the park, running around. I was in shock of where I was, so I asked my dad one final question. "Dad what can we do so that we can get out of here?"

"Unfortunately there is nothing we or anyone can do but pray. God will help us and take care of us."

Psalm 46:1 God is our refuge and strength, always ready to help in times of trouble.

As he was about to continue my mom hurried into the room.

"Oh there you are my son," my mom said, bursting into tears.

"What happened mommy? Why is your arm like that?" I asked, seeing her broken arm from the same crash that left me injured.

"Oh I'm going to be OK. Don't you worry about me," She said mournfully. "Let's just focus on getting you and your dad healthy and out of here."

"Where is Bicky?" I asked.

"He will be here soon. He is still walking down the hall. His leg is hurting a lot."

Minutes after my brother Ricky,(as I called him, Bicky when I was young) entered. He was on crutches, his leg in a cast, I asked him how he was doing. "Good" and he gave me a hug. "Oh Victor, I hope you will be better soon so that we can go play basketball."

"Me too," I replied, as tears rolled down my face. "Mommy, I want to go home now."

"First, you must get better I promise you, though, you will come home soon!"

My mom then went to my dad, starting to cry again as she bent over to kiss her husband.

"Gary don't worry. Everything will be OK. God will help our family."

"Thank you for the reminder Jessie that God is in control of all situations and He will take care of us."

As my mom talked to my dad trying to give him comfort, my mind kept trying to figure out how I got here in the first place. Was this all a dream or was it an ugly reality?

"Oh Victor," my mom said, "let me call the nurse so she can put some dry clothes on you. You shed so many tears that now your hospital gown is wet."

When my mom told me my first grade teacher would be coming to visit on the weekends, I couldn't remember who she was or my fellow classmates. I couldn't recall much of anything from before the crash.

As my mom was getting ready to leave, I pleaded with her to take me home.

"As soon as you get better. Until that day, we will come and visit every day. Just rest for now son and your dad is here with you. We'll see you tomorrow." She gave me another kiss and my brother gave me another hug.

When they left, silence filled the room. My dad said, "Oh my son be brave, courageous and keep holding on. God will be our strength. He will take care of us."

As my dad said those words of encouragement, I could not understand why this was happening to me. I could not understand why God was doing this to me. I just wanted to escape those four walls and get out of this hospital. Please somebody help me.

ECCLESIASTES 3

There is a time for everything,
and a season for every activity under the heavens:
a time to be born, and a time to die;
a time to plant, and a time to pluck up what is planted;
a time to kill, and a time to heal;
a time to break down, and a time to build up;
a time to weep, and a time to laugh;
a time to mourn, and a time to dance;
a time to throw away stones, and a time to gather stones together;
a time to embrace, and a time to refrain from embracing;
a time to seek, and a time to lose;
a time to keep, and a time to throw away;
a time to tear, and a time to sew;
a time to keep silence, and a time to speak;
a time to love, and a time to hate;
a time for war, and a time for peace.

My mom and dad before my brother and I were born. Healthy and free!

My brother and I. Young and Healthy.

My dad in the hills in India

It's A Beautiful Life

I was born on August 25,1977, in Punjab India, where temperatures could get to over 100 degrees during the summer. I was the second child, making me the baby in the family.

My mom was surrounded by family and friends at the time of my birth. My dad was not present at the time, he was in Chicago, Illinois going to the University to further his education and working as a security guard in a company that he hoped to excel at. My mom went to India to give birth to me was for insurance reasons. She was without insurance and it was cheaper for my birth to take place in India.

"Hi Honey the baby has finally arrived," my mom called once I was born. "He is healthy and weighs 8 pounds 12 ounces. What shall we name him?"

"How about Vikram? It is a name that rhymes or sounds so close to our eldest sons name Vikrant."

My mom agreed as my dad was so excited for my birth and couldn't wait to see me and hold me in his arms.

"We will come to Chicago in about 11 months from now. I just want Vikram to be able to spend time with his grandparents and relatives over here. Also it will give me time to spend with my family."

"OK dear, I will miss you until that day arrives that you and the children return and we can all be together again."

My dad lived to set good examples for our family to live by. Day in and day out he was either working during the day or going to the university in the evening so that he could build a bright future for his family.

He had gotten everything all set up and ready for our arrival. He had rented a one bedroom apartment, had bought warm clothes for the family since the weather in Chicago was cold in the winter months, and hot in the summer time. He was looking forward to our arrival.

After moving to the apartment we were very happy to be together and looked forward to the future. My parents prayed and hoped for the dreams, ambitions and desires for our family be fulfilled.

My mom would take both my brother and I for walks in the evening in the neighborhood. The neighbors adored us both, commenting on how cute we were. We also played in the house, parks, and the yard. All of us were so happy and felt so blessed.

My mom, my brother, and I enjoy the outdoors

All of us enjoying life in front of the lake where we lived in our one bedroom apartment.

My dad getting into his car to run some errands!

Welcome To The Windy City

On May 28, 1978, all of us were together in Chicago or sometimes called The Windy City.

My dad's sister Jassi lived in Chicago and was very helpful to lend us a hand. She had two children and a husband. We were a close-knit family who loved the outdoors. My dad was busy but he always managed to make time for the family. I can remember him telling me, when I was older, how tired he was from work and going to school. He attended the university three days a week.

Nevertheless, before he would leave for his studies in the university, he would play with my brother and I in the park close to our home. Even if it were only for half-hour, he would always devote that time and attention, to us.

The weather was a huge adjustment. In India, it was hot and cold but did not snow in the part of India where we lived. But winters in Chicago were rough. We had to bundle up with coats, long johns, mittens and boots before we would go out to play.

Money was tight with my mom not working. Our parents did not like to place us in child care where a stranger would take care of us. Yet, because we needed more income, my mom suggested that she work on the nights when my dad was not going to the university. That way, my dad could take care of us and no childcare would be necessary.

"OK that is a good idea. Thank you Jessie."

Our parents were such a good team. Always understood each other and knew how to coordinate tasks and help one another out.

One evening our mom put the cloth towels in the oven and tried to preheat the oven to cook something. When they were outside, talking to neighbors, they saw smoke coming out of the apartment windows. Our dad immediately ran inside to save both my brother and I who were sleeping in the bedroom.

"Oh thank God you two are safe," she said as she gave my brother and myself a hug.

"God saved us. Oh my gosh! What would my life be without both of you," my dad said.

My parents worked diligently to raise both of us in a loving environment, making sure we were properly taken care of every day. We were happy even though at times my dad got tired, working and going to school. He often dreamed of the day his studies would be completed. The light at the end of the tunnel as he would often say.

As the years went by, my dad graduated with a Masters in Business Administration

and was rewarded by the company.

"Honey I got a promotion and we are going to move to Kansas City, Missouri," he announced to the family.

"Oh wow that is great! What is the promotion?" my mom asked.

"It is an operational supervisor position. I will be in charge of hiring and firing of employees, overseeing my section which will be twenty five employees, and a lot bigger salary. It will be just where I want to be. Imagine no more dark circles under my eyes from going to school and working, plenty of time for the family, a bigger income, and a settled life. That's the kind of life we will have!" my dad said in a daze.

"Well then let's pack up our bags and get out of here. But first let's give thanks to God

Almighty for everything."

Thessalonians 5:18 Give thanks in all circumstances; for this is God's will for you in Christ Jesus.

All the boys in the family doing yard work!

Neighborhood gatherings were so wonderful in Missouri were the best!

My brother and I playing outside in the snow!

Family portrait taken two weeks prior to the crash that turned our lives upside down

Moving On

Once in Kansas City, we had great dreams, ambitions, and desires. Dreams of raising a family, dreams of having good health and dreams of being able to prosper for all of the years to come. Isn't that what everyone dreams of?

We started out by living in a two-bedroom apartment. We were well established, with my dad finally having his dream job, working as an operational supervisor. His job duties were to oversee his department which consisted of 25 employees and make sure it was running smoothly.

"It sure does feel great to be here in Kansas City Missouri and finally be working in the job that I have always wanted. Now I have a great job, great family, and a great life."

"Yes, thank God for all that we have," my mom said.

Psalm 92:1 It is good to praise the LORD, to sing praises to your name, O Most High.

During the day my dad worked and my mom stayed home to take care of us. He finally had a 9-5 job while my mom took care of the household duties and the two kids. We would go outside and play in the parks nearby or go swimming in the community pool down the street from where we lived.

At 5, I enrolled in kindergarten, one of 15 students, and Ms. Drysenstock was the teacher.

I was a good student who cooperated with the other children and made a lot of friends. I enjoyed learning and often was ahead of the class.

Ms. Drysenstock thought I would turn out to be a doctor or a lawyer as I was so smart.

My brother was in the third grade but in a different school. After school my mom would have a snack waiting for us and when my dad got home we would go to the parks that were close to our house to run around a bit.

Sometimes we were invited to neighborhood potluck parties. My mom often made Indian food that everyone enjoyed, rich with Indian spices. She cooked using a lot of cumin, masala, and other Indian herbs and spices.

On one occasion, when we arrived at the potluck party there were only three people whose names were Jim, Jan, and Robbie.

"Where should I put the food that I brought," asked my mom.

"Oh right over there on the kitchen counter will be fine. Here come let me help you Jessie,"

Jan replied.

My dad started to mingle, was very friendly and liked to strike up a conversation with anybody. He spoke with the host, Jim, telling him about his job, and how happy he was with his life.

"Sounds like you have the best of everything," Jim said.

"OK everybody soup's on. And dinner is being served," Jan announced.

After everybody got their food Jan led all of us in a little prayer before eating.

"Thank you LORD for this food and for this day that you have given to us. Thank you for all of the many people who have come to my house. Let our neighborhood remain strong with friendly people, good times and good health for everybody. Amen!"

Every day for an hour my dad would run on the track, close to our house. He ran to reduce the stress from work. He was about staying in shape and feeling good. My mom, brother and I would sometimes watch him run.

He constantly reminded us: "You must always follow a good diet and a good exercise routine to stay healthy and strong." He always encouraged us to play sports and stay active throughout his life.

Our dad's motto in life was "health is wealth." He was enjoying all that life had to offer. He had an awesome family life and a wonderful job that he worked so hard to achieve. Everything was perfect.

The Grewal Family
Victor Grewal (far left with arm cast) Injured
Gary Grewal (hospital bed) Injured
March 28, 1982

Two weeks after we took that family portrait taken in the previous chapter all of us were involved in a car crash caused by a drunk driver who turned our lives upside down. My dad and I were the ones who received the most severe injuries. March 28, 1982 will always remain a very sad day in history.

Lifes Unexpected Dives

"Hi honey, I am home from work," my dad said one Friday evening.

"Oh hi Gary. How was your day?"

"It was stressful. I had to fire one of my employees. Now when I return to work on

Monday I will have to look for a new employee to take her place. Never mind my day. How was your day?"

"It was good. I managed to clean the house while the kids were at school."

"Where are they now?"

"Oh they are upstairs in their room playing. Kids your daddy is home. Come on down," my mom said in a very loud voice.

My brother and I came running down the stairs. "Oh hi Daddy," we said in unison giving him a hug.

"How are my two little munchkins doing?" Dad asked.

"We are good."

"Your mom and I are very tired, kids. How about this evening all of us go out for a drive around town?"

"I need to get some stuff for the house from K-Mart. Let's stop by and get some cleaning supplies for the house," my mom said.

"OK so let's go for a little outing as well. A nice relaxing drive would be nice!," my dad said.

My brother and I ran down the stairs to the garage and our parents followed along.

"I get the front seat... I get the front seat...", I said.

"No you always get the front seat," my brother retorted.

"Kids, your mom gets the front seat. Both of you sit in the back seat. You, Vikram behind your dad and you, Vikrant, behind your mom on the right side of the car," he ordered.

To better assimilate into The U.S., we took more Americanized names. My dad became Gary, my mom, Jessie, my brother Ricky and I, Victor.

It was a white 1980 Ford Pinto my dad bought from the car dealership in Chicago. It sat four, equipped with AM/FM radio and seat belts. On this evening none of us were wearing seatbelts.

It was a chilly March evening with no hint of summer, still months away.

"Mommy I want a new toy," I said from the back seat.

"You already have enough toys in the house to play with son," my mom responded.

"Me too," my brother said.

"OK, well we'll see what we can find when we get to K-Mart," my dad replied.

"What a beautiful evening this is," my mom said

"Sure is. Kind of reminds me of Chicago during certain times of the year," my dad replied.

"Do you ever think of moving back there?," my mom asked

"Well my job is here now so I guess for now this is home for us. Beautiful Kansas City,

Missouri. The lakes are pretty and we are near parks for our children to play in and we have the best schools here. God has definitely blessed us with the best of everything," he said with a glance back in our direction.

Once at K-Mart, my brother and I ran around the store like crazy. We had a lot of energy.

"Mommy can I have this stuffed puppy dog?" I said. It was a little Pound Puppy. They were very popular back in the 80's.

"Well you have so many stuffed animals at home already."

"Pweeze mommy I love this puppy doggy!"

"OK then you can have it," my mom replied.

"How about me," my brother whined as he held a GI Joe in his hand.

"OK. OK, you may have the GI Joe," my parents told him.

As we were on our way out of the store, my brother begged our parents to buy him a chocolate chip cookie.

"Me too. Me too," I chimed in.

"You still have to eat your dinner. OK boys one chocolate cookie for each of you for after your dinner. You have to have it after dinner. Promise?" my parents asked.

We both nodded.

As my dad drove, my brother and I begged to have the cookie as we were very hungry. Our parents ended up giving us half of the cookie and saving the other half for dessert.

Everything was wonderful. My dad was whistling a tune he loved, my mom was feeling very content, and my brother and I were in the back seat making a mess, busily eating the half cookie our parents gave us. We made a turn less than two miles from our house.A drunk driver, high on marijuana and alcohol, ran a stop sign, plowing into our car. My mom was thrown from the car and landed on the street but her body kept rolling, by God's grace, only her arm was broken. My brother, still inside the car, broke his leg. My dad was left paralyzed, and I was left with a traumatic brain injury.

My brother was the only one who was conscious.

"Where is my purse," my mom cried, coming to after ten minutes.

"It is right here ma'am. Don't worry. It is safe. Your son is here by your side as well," said the paramedic treating her.

"Where is my husband and my other son?" my mom asked.

"I took care of them as well. Your son is in the other ambulance headed to the Children's

Hospital. We are headed for The Liberty Hospital where your husband and eldest son are being taken to."

Our dad was in a state of unconsciousness for two weeks. It was a shock when he finally awoke. I was unconscious for two months. Having lost all of the wonderful childhood memories I would wake up to a completely different life. Would I ever be able to get back to normal again?

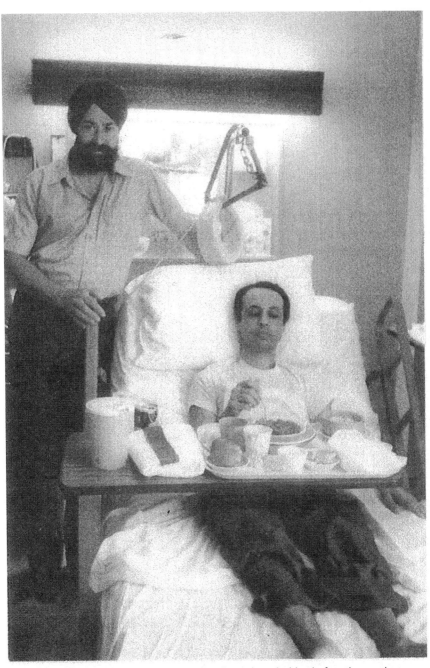

My dad left paralyzed and confined to a hospital bed after the crash.
Sadly, he never could walk again...

Health Is Wealth

I spent the first month at The Children's hospital in Kansas City, Missouri, lying motionless in a vegetated state. Not being able to do anything. With the help of machines to monitor my heart rate, feeding tubes to give me the nutrients I needed to keep me alive, my body was fighting just to stay alive. The only positive aspect of my experience: I did not know I was lonely and missing my family.

A month later, still unconscious, I was moved to Liberty Hospital. Now I was close to my family so when I awoke, at least I would have them by my side. I was taken to the same room as my father, who lay paralyzed, with a neck brace to keep his head straight.

My mom and brother had been released two weeks after the crash, their injuries were not as severe. As for my dad and I, only God knew how much time we would have to endure the feelings of loneliness, boredom, and sadness. Our only source of strength was prayer and God Almighty which is what my dad and I turned to many times in our desperation.

As I woke up from the coma, I was terrified, not knowing where I was.

"Hello... anybody... somebody please help me. I'm scared, dad."

"Hello... my son," a voice came from the other side of the room.

"Dad what are you doing in that bed over there? What am I doing in this bed over here? Come help me get out of this bed. I'm scared dad."

"I wish I could help you but now I cannot even help myself," he said, his voice quaking, with tears down his face.

I noticed how my right side of my body was able to move, not the left. It was totally motionless.

"Oh dad what happened to me? I cannot move the left side of my body." Could this be a dream...or is this an ugly reality?

"Oh my son, my darling son, you have finally woke up. Oh, I was so worried if you would wake up" my mom said walking quickly into the room. My brother was still down the hall, making his way slowly with crutches and a leg in a cast.

"What is that thing doing on your arm, mommy?"

"Oh this is just to help me get better," she responded in tears. "Don't worry about me. How are you my sweet Vikram?"

"I'm scared mommy. I want to go home!," I said as I started to cry.

"I know son, I know, I want you to come home too but first you must get well."

Just as my mom finished, my brother came to my bedside and gave me a hug. "Hi little bro... How are you? I wish we could play basketball like we used to. Remember?"

"No... I don't," I replied with tears rolling down my cheeks onto my hospital gown. "I want to go home," I told my brother.

"I want you to come home too and play games with you like we used to. We can go to the park and play and kick the soccer ball around."

While my brother was talking to me my mom was with my dad who was on the opposite side of the room.

"How are you doing Jasbir?"

"As good as can be... I am so happy that our little Vikram has finally woken up ," My dad said.

"Now all of us are back together again thanks to God Almighty," my mom replied.

"Yes. God will bring us through this. All we need to do is have faith," my dad said.

Corinthians 1:3 All praise to God, the father of our LORD Jesus Christ. God is our merciful Father and the source of comfort. He comforts us in all our troubles so that we can comfort others. When they are troubled, we will be able to give them the same comfort God has given us.

"Oh, my poor son Vikram. His life has just begun and look at what he has to deal with," my mom said as a tear ran down her face. "God will bring us through," she said, folding both hands and praying.

I only had one toy with me in the hospital, a Snoopy house, where Snoopy could move from the top to the bottom.

"Bicky, can you move the snoopy toy closer to me," I said as the snoopy toy was on the bedside table. He moved it closer to me.

As he made his way over to the side of my bed, I felt envious, imagining that someday I

would be able to be like him, to walk and not be confined to bed.

"OK son, we have to go now as I have to get your brother home to do his homework.

We will see you tomorrow after Vikrant's school is over."

"But don't leave me Mommy, I will be lonely."

"You have your dad here in the room with you. Don't worry son I will be back tomorrow."

"But I want you to stay here. I want all of us to stay together like a family."

"We are a family and someday all of us will be together at home. I have to go now and take care of your brother. I love you Vikram and will be back tomorrow, OK?"

"OK mommy, I love you too," I said, sobbing.

As my mom and brother left the room I opened and closed my eyes, seeing

if I could wake up from this nightmare.

"Oh son, what a life this is? I wish you did not have to go through all that you are going through now my son. Only God knows why this had to happen to us. As hard as it is, we must remember that God is with us and is going to take care of us. Let me teach you something about God, my son."

"OK," I said as I wiped away tears from my eyes.

"God is here but we cannot see him. We must have blind faith. Trust that God is going to take care of us and bring us through all of the hardships in life that we may face."

"How is there a God if I cannot see him?" I asked.

"We must believe and have faith. I wish I could read you the bible now, but with this neck brace, it is a bit difficult to do anything. Remember son, God is our comforter. He hears our cries and he is here with us at all times."

"Hi. How are both of you doing?", Doctor Miningrode, the primary doctor, said as she entered the room. She was thin in her mid 40's, with short, brown hair.

"As good as can be. I suppose," my dad said.

She walked over to dad and checked on his neck brace to make sure it fit properly and there were no problems.

"How are you Vikram?"

"I am here. I want to go home."

"You will as soon as you get better we will send you home. We have a lot of therapy sessions that you must attend that will make you stronger and help you to get better."

"Let me check on these feeding tubes to make sure it is working out good and everything is hooked up properly." She checked them, then said with a smile, "Looks like everything is working properly. I will be back later to check on you again tomorrow. Good night."

"Let's see what is on TV, son. There is only one TV so I guess we will have to watch one program only. What do you want to watch?"

"Cartoons," I replied.

"Let's see if there are any cartoons on at this time of the afternoon. Here is a Tom and Jerry cartoon."

As we watched Tom and Jerry, I was totally engrossed in the way Tom was trying to catch Jerry and It allowed my mind to shut out the outside world for a brief time, giving me a brief respite from my problems, trying to forget about my problems, trying to forget about yesterday's pains, and trying to remember God is always there.

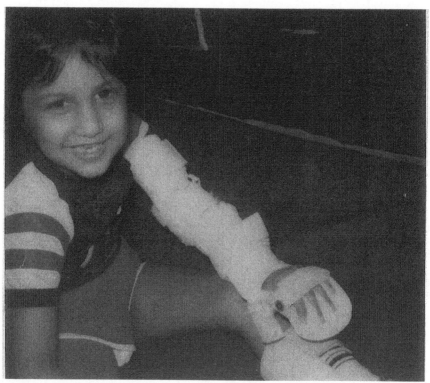

Trying to hide the pain that I felt I often smiled. This picture was taken in the rehab after a two month coma where I was given physical therapy hoping to get stronger.

Therapy For Life

One morning, a woman with brown hair, and medium height and with a big smile, entered my room. "Good morning. My name is Robin and I will be doing physical therapy with you three times a week to help you get strong again. I just wanted to introduce myself to you. I will see you this afternoon, OK. Someone will help you to come downstairs. I'll see you then."

After she left, my dad tried to encourage me. "Son, see you will be strong again and ready to take on the world."

"I don't want to go to therapy, Dad. I feel very weak and just feel like staying in my bed. I

cannot even move the left side of my body," I said feeling sad.

"Please try son! I know it will be hard but remember this, you must get up and try. The therapist will cheer you on as well."

"OK, I will try."

Just as I finished talking breakfast was being served to my dad. Eggs, toast, and orange juice. The aroma was appetizing. I was feeling so hungry as the feeding tubes I was put on was not curing my appetite. "I want some food please," I said to the attendant who served my dad.

"I will send the nurse in. I don't think I got a food order for you. Let me go and check on my cart."

"Oh, son, look at the life that we have to live. Don't get discouraged my son."

James 1:12 God blesses those who patiently endure testing and temptation. Afterward they will receive the crown of life that God has promised to those who love him.

After breakfast, my dad had to undergo painful catheterization. It was the only way that he could empty his bladder since everything from the chest down did not work, except for his arms. Afterwards, we prayed a lot, when the TV shows got boring.

"OK Vikram, time to go to your very first therapy session. Let's start getting ready," Lilllian the CNA took off my hospital gown, removed the feeding tubes, put my clothes on, transferred me to the wheelchair and then pushed me to the therapy room. It was a lot to endure for therapy.

I was scared the first time I saw the therapy room. There were so many injured people trying to get better. There were monkey bars, motorized bicycles, treadmills, and mats. It looked like a mini gym.

"OK Vikram, I will leave you at this table. The therapist will be here in a few minutes." Minutes later, a tall, slender woman with light brown hair arrived.

"Hi Vikram. It is very nice to meet you. My name is Cassandra and I am going to be your therapist today. How are you?"

"I am nervous," I said, imagining how hard all of the exercises would be.

"Don't be nervous. I am just going to do a few exercises to help make you strong again. We have to make a brace for your left arm today, as it is weak.

As I waited, I got even more nervous and panicky. "I want to go back to my bed. I am scared."

"Honey, calm down. Everything is going to be OK. Now look, I have this cloth that I am going to wrap around your arm when I wet it in this tub of warm water. OK here we go."

As she gently rolled the cloth around my arm, I could feel the plaster harden. But my muscles kept tightening up and it felt very uncomfortable. The mold of my arm was not coming out correctly.

"OK we have to start over again. Can you try to just relax your muscles because that was extracting the mold and it was not coming out right."

"OK I'll try."

As she wrapped my arm with the lukewarm cloth, I concentrated to relax, telling my muscles to not tighten up.

"OK, now in a few minutes we will take this mold off. Just relax."

I tried the best I could to not let my arm tighten up and just relax. It was extremely challenging but this time, the mold came out perfect.

"OK Vikram, now we are going to get down on the mat and do some leg exercises. Now I am going to assist you to pick your left leg up and down. As she moved my leg, I had painful spasms, but as she kept moving it, the spasms lessened. We worked on this for about five minutes, then got me back in my wheelchair.

Next we went to the table where she had me do a few arm and hand exercises. She gave me a tennis ball to squeeze. I tried but was unable to accomplish much. "This is too hard for me to do," I said in frustration.

"OK. Our therapy session is over and you did a really good job."

As she pushed me back up to my room, my mind kept racing. Thoughts of all of the hard work and perseverance I would need to put in to get my health back had my mind struggling to find answers. How long would I need therapy? When I get my arm brace, would that make my left hand normal again? Then, would I be able to use it and would it function correctly? So many questions that only God knew the answers to.

Isaiah 40:31 But those who wait for the LORD shall renew their strength, they shall mount up with wings like eagles, they shall run and not be weary, they shall walk and not faint.

As I got back to my room, my dad asked me how therapy went.

"It was good but hard. I will get an arm brace in a week."

"Do you want to watch anything on TV, son?"

"OK, put on some cartoons I guess," I said feeling very bored.

"OK, but first, can I pray for you, son? Let's both say a prayer. Let's ask God for support and strength for only he is our ultimate support in all of the trials in our lives.

Psalm 72:13 He has pity on the weak and needy, and saves lives of the needy.

"OK son, fold your hands and close your eyes," my dad instructed before he began praying for both of us.

"Dear heavenly father I pray that you help us to go home soon and to return to good health. I pray that you help my son to live a fulfilled life where he can succeed in all that he does and let all that he do be in honor to you. Amen,".

I was still feeling sad, so after he finished, I asked him, "If there is a God, then why is he not sending me home now?"

"You will learn as you get bigger and more mature that God has a plan. I am frustrated too. We must wait upon the Lord and have patience for only he knows about our past, present, and of what is to come. God has kept all of us alive, hasn't he? He could have killed all of us in that awful crash."

"Yes. This is too much for me dad! I would rather be dead."

"Oh son, I feel so bad for you," he said as tears rolled down his face. "We just need to hold on. Please son have faith, courage, and God will bring us through this.

A few hours later, my dad was being served dinner and I woke up to the smell of chicken and vegetables.

"OK, here is your dinner, Mr. Grewal. Do you have everything that you need?" the attendant said.

"Yes," everything is good. Thank you very much," my dad replied.

"Oh dad, I am very hungry and the food that you are having smells so good."

But my dad quickly replied that the food wasn't as good as it smelled, that he made food much more delicious when he was healthy and at home. He added that he hoped he would be home soon.

"Hopefully, that day will come again soon, daddy." I added.

"Yes, we will continue to pray.

Philippians 4:19 And my God will fully satisfy every need of yours according to his riches in glory in Christ Jesus.

Nurses awoke my dad and I several times during the night to make sure that we were OK. It was very irritating but this was the routine that the hospital used to regularly monitor their patients.

The next day, I was given speech therapy to focus on strengthening the muscles in my mouth. We would work on having proper lip closure so when I made words such as mom,

tom, mop etc., I would be able to speak clearly. All of the words that required both the upper and bottom lip to close was very difficult for me.

"Hi my name is Sally. I am going to give you speech lessons to help you work on those vocal muscles. I am going to hold up these flash cards. Please try to pronounce these words." First she held up a picture of a mop. "Can you say mop."

I tried and tried. The way I said mop did not sound quite right.

"OK, let's work on some of these lip-closure exercises. Close your upper and bottom lip. Let's try to do this 10-15 times."

It took a lot of strength out of me and was so difficult to do.

"OK, let's see if we can match these pictures and say the name of the picture out loud."

I looked at the pictures. I picked two pictures that looked alike. All of these pictures were of fruits that forced me to make proper lip closure.

"Vear, vanana", I said.

" OK repeat after me. P...P...P... can you make that sound? b... b... b... can you make that sound?"

We had a 30 minute therapy session and were to continue the following week with all of these exercises with proper lip closure. It was difficult for me having to learn how to do everything all over again. I was given speech therapy to help me talk clearly and physical therapy to regain my strength every day. I would continue to do this for the rest of my life.

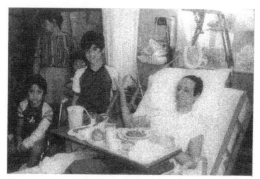

As a family with a life that had been turned upside down by a drunk driver, hope was all we held on to.

My family took me outside of the hospital room outside for a break. Here my uncle is holding me in his arms.

My first grade teacher visited me often and made me smile.

Will I Ever Go Home?

The biggest question that I had while rehabilitating was: Will I ever go home?

Days seemed too tough and nights seemed too long as I waited to see what God's will would be? What direction would he lead me to? All I had to do was trust in the LORD that everything would be alright.

"Hello gentlemen. How are you doing today," Dr. Miningrode asked as she walked in the room one morning Dad was eating his breakfast.

I looked up at her with a face of desperation. "What's going to happen today? Am I going to go home?"

"No Vikram you have a while until you get better and you are still on feeding tubes."

"Oh I want to go home so bad," I cried.

"Just hang in there. Your brother and mother should be coming in today to visit soon," she said as she tried to comfort me.

"Hi Jasbir. How are you?"

"As good as I can be I suppose. I have one question, do you think I will ever be able to walk again?"

Her answer was blunt and to the point. "No."

His heart and spirit sank as he shed a tear. I cried along with my dad, feeling hopeless, caught up in all this mess. Everything seemed to me like a tangled web. How to untangle it was a big question in my mind.

"Oh son whatever I must have done to deserve this? At least I have you here with me. We are a team Vikram. I will walk again son, you wait and see. Until that day, we must continue to pray and ask God for his protection. Don't worry son. We will get through this but first we must get out of this hospital."

"Dad can you turn on the TV? Let's see what's on."

We turned on "The Wizard of Oz," a classic.

"How about this movie son? This is a good movie."

It was a great movie with such wonderful characters that were brought to life. As Dorothy tapped her little red shoes in the movie and repeated, "There's no place like home. There's no place like home." I kept thinking to myself if I could stand on my own and tap my feet together I would go back home. Home to where I could have freedom to be a kid. It would be fun to take a walk in the park or to spend time with my mom and brother and never say goodbye, like now when they would come to visit. My imagination was running wild. It felt good to think of all of these things. The painful part was waking up to reality. Just as I stopped daydreaming my mom and brother entered the room.

"Hello Vikram how are you doing today?"

"I can't wait to start eating. These feeding tubes are not doing good."

"Oh honey I know, but we will have to wait until the doctor says you can have solid foods."

"This is too much for me mommy. I want to go home and play with Bicky in the house. I want you to stay here with me mommy," I said holding her close.

All of us started to whimper and then cry. "OK my sonny. Everything will be OK. Don't worry. Your kindergarten teacher Ms. Drysenstock should be here later on today. She has been so busy with work and feels bad she has not been able to come in to see you."

How can anyone be too busy not to call or not to visit, when I am the one who is suffering?

Doesn't anyone want to see me? I thought this many times during my days in the hospital.

The next day came and I went therapy. Cassandra, was waiting for me too as I was assisted to go downstairs by Kathleen, the morning Certified Nursing Assistant.

"I got your hand brace ready for you to use. Here it is. Let's see how it fits?"

After Casandra made the proper adjustments, the brace fit perfectly. At least that's what I thought before starting the exercises.

"Now, I want you to wear this all the time. It will help to make your hand and arm better. Please try and wear it all the time."

"I will try," I promised.

"OK, now let's go to the table to do some arm exercises."

As she took me to the table, my arm started to tighten up, encased in the brace.

"Ouch my hand hurts wearing this brace. Please take it off," I said as my hand started to spasm.

"OK. OK", she said undoing the Velcro that was keeping my arm in the brace.

"Oh that scared me. My hand never did that before."

"Now, relax your hand. When you're ready, try to squeeze this ball in your left hand ten times."

I slowly picked up the ball using my left hand and squeezed the ball three times before I got tired.

It was so discouraging, since I was unable to get up to 10 as she requested.

I asked if we could move on.

Next exercise was for the leg. Casandra instructed me to grab the bars next to my wheelchair.

"Can you try to pull yourself up?"

I did and took a few steps before falling, crying uncontrollably.

"OK, Vikram, that's all for the therapy for today. Next time, we will work more on walking and hand exercises. How about a great, big happy face sticker for today?"

I returned to my room. Ms. Drysenstock, my kindergarten teacher, was talking to my dad while waiting for me.

"Surprise Vikram! I am finally here. I decided to take a whole day off just so I could come visit you. I want to let you know how much all of us miss you in our classroom and hope that you will be able to come back soon."

"I hope to come back to school also."

While the nurse put me back in bed and hooked up the IVs and feeding tubes, Ms. Drysenstock asked if I remembered any of my classmates, rattling off their names. I couldn't remember anyone.

"All of us are praying for you and hope you get back to full and complete health. I am not used to seeing you like this. If there's anything I can do for you, please tell me," she said, giving me a hug as she started to cry.

"Can you visit me more?"

"I will try. School is so busy now but I promise that I will try to come and visit you every weekend when school is not in session. You keep strong, Vikram, and please, never give up."

Day in and day out, this was the life I had for seven months. It was like a prison cell for me that I had no way to escape. I was tired of the doctors, nurses, and visitors telling me how much they missed me, tired of all of the long, painful therapy sessions. All I wanted to do was go home. I'd had enough and wanted to give up.

But God kept my dad and I strong, and finally it was time to go home. I was able to walk a few steps but mostly had to stay in the wheelchair. I was happy to leave the hospital but wondered what would await me outside of that building. What kind of life would I have?

It was one of the happiest days of my life. I was so excited to see what God had in store for me.

Yet, while I was leaving, my dad still had a few months of hospitalization ahead of him. I was sad that he couldn't come home with me but at least I was released from this prison.

ALL BECAUSE OF A DRUNK DRIVER! PLEASE DON'T DRINK AND DRIVE!

Mom posing for a photo in the family room where
my dad's hospital bed was

My mom taking a well deserved break to lay down and rest after
taking care of the family

Dad confined to a wheelchair having lunch at the dining room table.
My older brother in the family room watching TV

Adaptations

Driving home, I felt happy and excited, yet sad that my dad was still in the hospital.

"Oh boy mommy, I am so happy and content to finally be free. Look at all the trees and birds in the trees. I have never seen anything like it," I said with excitement.

"Oh, my son, there is a lot that you still have yet to see."

The drive home was a very happy time for me. As we arrived, I waited for my mom to take my wheelchair out of the trunk of the 1980 Oldsmobile that my mom had purchased after the crash. My legs were skinny with a brace to help me walk, a brace on my left arm and a wheelchair to get around in. As she transferred me from the car to the wheelchair, I could feel a sense of relief. I was finally home.

I sat in the garage for a while as my mom had brought me a can of juice, we reflected on the last nine months I was away from the house.

"Victor, we missed you so much and just want you to know how much you were missed.

Do you remember anything of this house?"

"No not really. I do not remember anything."

"I will help you get up and down the stairs, OK son? Your bedroom is on the right side of your brother's bedroom and there is a bathroom very close by."

I had noticed many puppies and kittens on the street and asked if I could have one or the other.

My mom replied patiently, "All that will come. First, we have to settle down."

I asked what "settling down" meant.

"Son, all of us have been through a lot and life is kind of like starting all over again. Your dad still has to come home, too. Then I will have to help him, you and your brother as everyone will be needing help. Oh son, how I wish this crash had never happened and things could have been different. Oh well, all we have to remember that God is in control of everything and you are finally home. I am thankful for that."

As we left the garage, I tried to walk on my own, holding on to my mom's waist. I got as far as two steps before telling her that was all I could do and then I fell.

"Can you crawl a bit Victor?"

I got down on my knees and had a bit of a problem crawling to the steps to go to the first floor of the house since the left side of my body was weak.

"Oh, look, stairs going down the house," I said with some excitement.

"Yes, that is the basement. I will help you go down there later. Let's see, can you sit on the steps and bump yourself up?"

I gave it a try, bumping my way up the steps, one at a time. It wasn't easy, as I had to support my weight.

"Oh, this is hard Mommy. Can you help me?" I said, struggling just to keep my balance while I was sitting on the steps. The left side of my body did not support me at all.

"OK son, here we go." She held me from under my armpits and lifted me to the highest step. OK try to stand up Vikram," she said feeling a bit tired.

I managed to stand up and take a few steps but then fell, telling her how hard it was for me to do.

She assisted me to get into a chair that was close to the dining room, then went to cook dinner, allowing me to rest.

The food was delicious, especially to me. I felt good to be able to eat solid food. What a blessing from God Almighty to not be fed through feeding tubes. The food would give me strength to grow stronger and stronger.

One of my biggest ambitions in life was to be like everyone else. As a child, I wanted to be able to run around with all of the kids in my neighborhood and wanted to participate in all of the games or activities. But many times I was on the outside looking, much like Rudolph the red nose reindeer since I was not like other kids. It was a constant struggle for me but I knew if I had faith in God Almighty, he would make my dreams come true.

Psalm 16:8 I know the LORD is always with me. I will not be shaken, for he is right beside me.

That night, I felt so happy and content laying in my own bed with a big teddy bear that my mom had bought for me as a welcome-home gift. I could finally say, "Thank you God I am finally home."

God only knew what struggles everyday would bring. Making friends, adapting to a new school, having the strength to climb all of the stairs in the house.

JOB 9:10 He does great things too marvelous to understand. He performs countless miracles.

The next day I awoke, feeling surprised and overjoyed to not be in the hospital. I felt as if my heart was dancing. I slowly got out of bed. My mom was already downstairs cooking breakfast for my brother and I. I tried to walk a few steps, but fell. I crawled to the stairs and slid down to living room then crawled again to the kitchen, five or ten steps away.

"Good morning my dear Vikram. How are you? Here let me help you get into a chair," she said as she lifted me onto a chair.

"Mmm... That looks so good," I said as I was watching my brother eat homemade pancakes with butter and syrup.

"Your plate is coming up too son. This is your first breakfast at home. I wanted to surprise you!"

"Mmm... It is so good mommy," I said as she put the plate in front of me and took a big bite.

"Happy son?"

"Yes, very happy," I replied with a big smile on my face.

"Good, today the plan of the day is go visit your father as he must be very lonely in that hospital. While your brother is in school that is what we will do."

"Really, mom? I don't want to go back to the hospital. I don't like that place. It brings back bad memories."

"Vikram we have to. Remember how much you enjoyed it when your brother and I would visit every day."

As my mom and I went to visit my dad, I felt a little upset, going back to the prison.

"Hi son, how are you?" my dad said as mom pushed me in my wheelchair into the room "How is life at home. I sure do miss you son. Hopefully, I will be able to go home as well."

I noticed his neck brace was gone and when I mentioned it, he said he was still having difficulty turning his neck.

"Gary how are you feeling?" my mom asked.

"I am feeling OK. I just miss being at home and miss everyone so much. Especially I miss my little son Vikram. Oh, I pray for him every night and pray that he be courageous in this life and be victorious. Just as his name means Victorious."

I told him I was strong. And to prove it, I flexed my right arm, doing a decent impression of Popeye The Sailor Man.

"OK Jasbir, so now we must get the house ready for you. There are stairs in the house so we will need to get a wheelchair lift so I can take you upstairs to the bathroom. And from the garage to the family room.

"I think my bed should go in the living room. That way when I want to go outside then I will only have to be taken down one flight of stairs. It will be easier," my dad said.

"I will also have to have a specialized bathroom made for you where your wheelchair can go in and out of. It will probably be attached to our room upstairs," my mom said.

"How does Vikram do in the house now? Does he get around pretty good?"

"He does the best he can. He does have trouble getting up and down the stairs but he manages it pretty well. He just sits on the stairs and bumps his way up and down."

"We've also have to enroll him in a school but will require special education because of his short term memory deficit. We will find a school for him to go to," my dad said.

We talked for the next few hours of the adaptations we would have to make. It was not going to be easy for any of us, but was something that needed to be done. There would need to be wheelchair lifts to assist my dad, a specialized bathroom to be installed, a hospital bed for him, not to mention all the necessary medical supplies.

My mom's life was so full, taking care of the family. On top of all of the preparation for my dad to return home, there was the added responsibility of having to taking care of two young boys. Her plate was overflowing but she always told me God is in control of everything and God will help us.

That night, my mom made a blueprint in her mind of where everything would fit once my dad was home.

"Let's see, the hospital bed will go where this couch is. Up here, the bathroom will be constructed. Down here, we will keep some exercise equipment for all of us to use.

Before going to bed that night, she told me, "Vikram, I can't believe you are home. That means that you have gotten better. I thank God Almighty for that every day! You are a brave boy to have gone through all that."

Psalm 9:1 I will give thanks to the LORD with my whole heart; I will tell all your wonderful deeds.

As I was put to bed, I asked, my mom, "Mommy when will daddy come home?"

"He will come soon my son. Very soon. I don't know when. Only God knows the answer to that question. You miss your dad, huh Vikram?"

"Yes I do," I replied with a tear running down my cheek. Starting to sob, I asked, "Why us? Why are we the ones who are suffering?"

"God will take care of all of us. You just wait and see." She kissed me on the cheek as she began to read me a bedtime story. As I fell asleep and she whispered, "Good night my son, sweet dreams."

The next day brought fresh beginnings, new horizons, and unknown adventures.

As I ate breakfast with my brother, then saw him get ready for school, I was just a bit jealous. My brother was riding a bike to school. Why couldn't I?

"Mommy I want to learn how to ride a bicycle and go to places on my bike".

"Someday you will son," she assured me. "Right now, you need to get stronger. You just now had a major injury. We'll have to spruce this house up and get it ready for your dad so when he comes home we will all be together again".

As my mom was busy doing everything to help the family out, I saw, a Jane Fonda workout record. As she turned on the record and began her workout routine, I tried to follow along, using the left side of my body as much as I could.

"Left arm up, right arm up. Lift it higher, getting stronger," Fonda's voice commanded, guiding the workout.

"That's good for you. You are doing a very good job, Vikram," my mom said, watching me from the family room.

Soon I got tired and was unable to do anymore. My mom turned off the record player and I
laid on the couch and fell asleep.

My mom was busy all day, making calls to various places. The neighbors helped out, giving her a hand moving the couch from the family room to the basement, a job she couldn't have managed herself.

Later that day, we called the hospital to check on my dad.

After I asked how he was doing, his answer saddened me.

"Oh I am having a party," he said sarcastically, "What do you think I am doing. There's nothing much that I can do except wait till my time comes for me to get out of this damn place!"

After I began crying, my mom took the phone from me.

"Jasbir how are you? Is everything OK?"

"Yes, sorry I am getting frustrated stuck here in this hospital bed."

"Well all we can do is hope and pray that you be released soon and able to come home. Oh, I wish you could walk out of that hospital and come home now."

"Yes, but we do have to accept reality and just know that God is in control, only he knows why we are going through this.

Jeremiah 29:11 "For I know the plans I have for you," declares the LORD, plans to prosper you and not harm you, plans to give you hope and a future."

She then related to him all the plans she was making for the day when he would come home. It was something he understood, yet the frustration was understandable.

As my mom hung up the phone after talking to my dad, tears came rolling down her face, as she remembered the time when everything was OK.

Months passed and everything was done; specialized bathroom constructed, furniture moved, hospital bed ordered. Now all we were doing was waiting for my dad.

First Christmas after the crash. Thankful to be home
Thankful to be home I always had a smile on my face!

Homecoming- All Together Again

After being alone for three months in the hospital, my dad finally came home.

On the day we picked him up, the hospital provided us with a sliding board, in order to more easily move him from the wheelchair into the car.

"Ah finally I am going home today," he said as we gathered up his possessions.

"I sure am happy that you are coming home, Jasbir," my mom said.

"So am I Jessie. I've been asking God for this day to arrive soon. We will finally be one family under one roof. It will be hard and challenging as now we will have to make a lot of adaptations for me, and the children need help too but if that is what life brings then let it be. We can handle it."

On arriving home, my dad thought back to the evening we went to K-Mart and what he thought was going to be a most enjoyable ride.

"What are you thinking about Jasbir?" my mom asked, as we arrived noticing he was in deep thought.

"Oh I was just remembering how all of us left to go out that evening. We were so tired from all of the day's activities and wanted to get out and relax. And look what happened!" he said, tearing up. "I'm sorry honey."

"Don't be sorry Jasbir and don't even look back. All we must do is look forward and keep our eyes what the future holds for us as a family."

"You are right," he said sighing.

When my mom got out of the car she asked me to try to get out of the car, standing close by for support. I stood up, took a few steps but lost my balance and fell. My mom brought my wheelchair and pushed me next to where my dad was sitting.

"Hi my little son," he said as he laid his left hand on my right shoulder. "How are you?"

"I am doing good. I am happy to have you home dad. No more hospital for us," I said.

"Yes, I am very happy son. No more doctors and nurses to bother us anymore. We will live this life the best that we can. We will have struggles and limitations, but God will help us and take care of us. We must give thanks to God Almighty for bringing us this far. Look how far we have come my son."

"I know dad," I said shedding more tears.

My dad had to be taken up to the family room by a machine that his wheelchair was hooked up to. At first, he was fearful that the wheelchair would come loose and he would fall out. But as months passed, he became more trusting since he was using it four times a day.

First thing in the morning, upstairs to the bathroom, then back downstairs to his bed. After lunch, down to the garage where he would do his exercises and, at the end of the day, back up to the family room.

While he liked to be as independent as possible, he would have to ask my mom for assistance. It created quite a strain on my mom.

Many times I can remember her trying to do more than one thing at a time. There was no time to sit down and relax. She started to get up very early to pray to God, asking him for strength to do everything as she had to help all of us. Sometimes she would start to cry as it became overwhelming to have to do everything all by herself.

"I need help Jasbir. Can we please hire someone to help us out so I could have more energy and not be so tired. Taking care of you and the kids is very hard," she said weeping one day.

"No I can do everything by myself," My dad replied. "We do not need any help."

"Please Gary you do not understand. I am so tired and need some help. Vikram can hardly walk, Ricky needs to be taken places and needs to do things that require my attention. You

have to be taken up and down the stairs various times everyday! Please Jasbir I need help,"

she said crying as she gave my dad a hug.

"OK OK, I understand... we will start to look for someone," my dad agreed.

"Yes that would be good. Maybe someone to help me two times a week."

"OK dear, if that is what you really need then we need to start looking."

"Thank you Jasbir for your understanding."

That night, watching the evening news, we saw a car crash that occurred on the freeway that was very close to our home.

The news report said a drunk driver crashed into another car the previous night, killing four passengers. The driver was found four times the amount of alcohol in his system above the legal limit.

"Look at all of this nonsense! Sometimes I just feel like turning the TV off or changing the channel. Why do people decide to drink and drive? It is something that I can never figure out. The laws need to be more strict for drunk drivers to get off the roads or else families will continue to suffer. Just look how much all of us are suffering....and that drunk driver who was high on marijuana and alcohol got just a $75.00 fine," he fumed after watching the news report.

"Yes, that is true," my mom responded. "The laws do need to be more strict."

I write this from the recollection of my memory of what my dad told me. I was too young to remember anything, and what happened to the drunk driver. My dad just told me that he was given a $75.00 fine and he was very upset at what he had done when all of us went to court.

The next day really pushed my mom to the limit.

It started when I awoke with dizziness and a temperature that spiked way above normal. I managed to get to my moms room to wake her with my complaints.

Then, she had to wake my brother to get him ready for school. And my dad needed a cup of tea.

As I lay in bed resting, I felt really bad for my mom who was trying to juggle around all of these different tasks just to make the family happy.

Psalm 34:18 The LORD is near to the brokenhearted, and saves the crushed in spirit.

My mom made my dad a cup of tea, and ran upstairs to check to see if my forehead was still hot. Then, I could hear my parents talking to one another as my dad was being transported up the stairs with the help of the wheelchair lift.

"Oh Gary I have made up my mind. I am going to call someone to help us out during the day. I cannot do this all by myself."

"I just don't want anyone to see all of my medical supplies. I don't want them to see me like this." He said as he was filled with pride. "I can do everything on my own anyways"

"What everything? I am running around this house doing everything, taking care of everyone and not even having any time for myself." They argued a bit but eventually agreed to get part-time help for my mom.

My dad managed to use the bathroom independently. Took him quite a while to do everything because he had to transfer so much. To brush his teeth, shave, transfer to the toilet, transfer back to the wheelchair, transfer to the shower chair, take a shower, then transfer back to the wheelchair was not easy. It strained his arms and made him tired. After all was done he called my mom who then transferred him downstairs to the hospital bed where she would serve him his breakfast. He would also watch TV and get ready to get out of bed which took him a few hours. It was a very hard lifestyle since he was so dependent on my mom for help and had to adjust to a new way of living.

Later that day when my dad was in the garage doing his exercises my mom got a reference of a cleaning woman from one of the neighbors.

The neighbor, Danny, told my mom this woman was very dependable and always on time. It was a strong, positive recommendation. Danny had noted how stressed my mom had become and was concerned, telling her, "If you need anything else, please let me know."

My mom called the reference, Evelyn, who agreed to come over the next day and discuss what my mom needed. She was told there was a paralyzed man along with two young boys. When my father found out, he was extremely unhappy.

"Jessie what are you trying to do? I told you that I do not want anyone because of my medical supplies and I don't want anyone to see me like this."

"I need help, don't you understand. I cannot do everything by myself!"

"OK, whatever, Jessie. Can you please take me back upstairs?" My dad demanded angrily.

As my mom hooked my dad up to the machine she had tears running down her face.

"Oh, only God can help me," she said to herself. As she gave all of us our dinner, finished putting my brother and I to bed, helped my dad to lay down in bed, she felt exhausted from all of the work she was doing for the family.

Psalm 91:1 Those who live in the shelter of the Most High will find rest in the shadow of the Almighty.

The next day my brother and I got ready for school.

My brother always managed to be able to get dressed faster than I could. I could never understand why but after a while I came to realize for me, everything in life would take longer to complete such as simple tasks like getting dressed and putting on my socks and shoes, learning new material in school, homework, everything.

School was a challenge for me since I had problems with my short term memory after the crash. That makes remembering information in the short term challenging and why I was in special education. It bothered me and was something I did not like. I wanted to be like everyone else but many times was teased and did not fit in with the activities that other kids of my age were doing. Not even the simplest of things like walking straight or using my left hand to full extent. I had to learn how to do everything with one hand. I learned how to put on socks, getting dressed and many other things with one hand. That's why, for many years, I only wore shoes with velcro instead of laces that I could just fasten tightly with my right hand.

I was constantly reminded by my parents, teachers, school counselors and other people that if I wanted to get strong again the only way would be to use the left side of my body as much as I could. My second grade teacher kept reminding me to try to keep my left hand on the desk to hold the paper with my left hand and write with my right hand. It was difficult as my left hand would end up sliding off the desk. I sometimes thought the left side of my body had a mind of its own.

At home, there were also frustrations for me.

"Vikram can you please try to hold the plate with your left hand as you wash it?" my dad would say.

"OK I will try," I replied.

"Vikram can you please try to remember what I am trying to teach you of how to say your

ABC's," my dad would ask me. One time he slapped me very hard as I could not remember his instruction of how to remember my ABC's. He did not yet know of my short-term memory deficit which made remembering any kind of instruction hard to remember. My long-term memory was not affected.

My dad would teach me the ABC song but after only one minute I would forget.

"A B C D E. Let's try to repeat the alphabet."

"A B C D F G I".

"No son, what's wrong with you son that is about the fiftieth time I have told you. Now for heaven's sake remember A B C D E F. Now repeat it!!! "

I started to cry in frustration.

It seemed as if no one could understand me. I felt alone and confused, many times not knowing what to do? I often asked questions to my parents every day of how to deal with everything that life was presenting to me. Their answer was always one simple answer. "My son, depend on God Almighty and everything will be OK."

Lamentations 3:22-23 The faithful love of the LORD never ends! His mercies never cease. Great is his faithfulness; his mercies begin afresh each morning.

Always smiling... always trying to shine. After every downhill dive,
my smile always brought me back up! 2nd grade picture

Trying to fit into the classroom with all of the special needs students was hard but
nothing would take away the smile that God had given to me...

Fitting In

Every day I was trying to improve myself, trying to be like everyone else but it wasn't easy. One day I went downstairs, put on my Velcro shoes, and walked outside to try to play tag with the kids in the street but was kicked out of the game since I could not move very fast. I was even pushed to the ground by one of the kids who tagged too hard.

I lost my balance, fell and ended up with bruises on my arms and legs. I cried and cried, prompting my mom to come out to see what happened.

"Oh, my son, what happened."

"Mommy, I tried to play and fell down."

"Oh, my poor son. Let me take you inside and put a bandage on these wounds. Oh son don't ever try to play with the other kids. You may get hurt like you did just now. If you would have gotten more severely hurt, imagine what that would have caused me. I cannot take any more pressure than I already am dealing with. Your brother or I will take you for a ride in your wheelchair everyday to give you a break from being stuck in all day."

"Now mommy? Now, can I go for a ride in my wheelchair? Can you take me for a ride?"

"Jessie I need your help," my dad called from his hospital bed.

"I have to help your dad now. Maybe a little bit later I will have time to take you for a ride."

"OK," .... "But all I want to do is have a little bit of fun."

As she ran down the stairs to see what my dad wanted I sat in my room on my bed. Looking at all of the kids playing on the neighbor's driveway and in the street, I felt like Rudolph The Red Nose Red Nosed Reindeer who was left out of all of the games. I even turned on my Teddy Ruxpin so I would have someone who could talk to me. I would also talk back, imagining that it could hear me.

"OK son, your father is in the garage doing his exercises for the day. He wants to talk to you.

"OK mommy," I said as I wiped away the tears from my eyes.

As she helped me to get down the stairs I continued to cry all the way to where my dad was.

"Hi son. How are you doing? Have a seat next to me.

She drove to the grocery store, giving me and my dad a chance to talk.

I was still whimpering when my dad put down the Bible he was reading and asked, "Son, how are you?"

"Sad very sad. Oh how I try daddy. I try to stay strong. I try to depend on God alone. Even though I cannot see God I try to depend on him."

"Yes son, we must depend on God Almighty because he will take care of us. Look at me stuck here in this wheelchair not understanding why I am going through all that I am going through. Believe me son, a lot of times I just want to give up. This book here called The Bible is the greatest book. You are too young to understand now my son, but as you grow older you will see how God is in control of everything and how we must depend on God alone. Here let me read you some scriptures from the bible. It will strengthen us and give us faith," he said as he gave me a hug.

"Oh be strong my son. It breaks my heart to see you going through such misery. The light is God Almighty. So let's turn to the Almighty word."

He then related the story of Job. He had everything in life. He had many children, animals, and servants. He was very rich. Satan took away everything, leaving him helpless. God presented him with many tests but in the end got back everything and much more.

"In the same way son, this may be a test that we are going through to test our faith in him. We must have 100 percent faith in God Almighty and that he will take care of us in all of the ups and downs in life. Our life has been turned into a roller coaster. Our life took a deep unexpected dive. Now all of us must hold on tight and have faith in God Almighty."

As he told me those very comforting words my mind couldn't comprehend it. All I wanted to do was have fun, to run around in the parks and play with all the children. I wanted my dad to somehow start to walk, so then we could play like other children in the neighborhood did with their fathers.

"OK son, now I will read you a very powerful passage in the bible. Peter 5:7 'Give all your worries and cares to God for he cares about you.'

This means that God cares for you and will help you. Do not depend on anyone else but God Almighty. See my son, you and I are a team. Let's depend on God Almighty and let's stay strong. We should support one another through all of the hardships we face as there will be many. You and I son are in the same boat. Helpless and relying on God for support."

Just as he said those final words my mom came home with loads of groceries. My brother also came home from playing with his friends.

"Daddy, someday I want to be able to run around like Bicky."

"You will son. We just have to patiently wait and God will supply us with all of our needs."

Philippians 4:19 And the same God who takes care of me will supply all of your needs from his glorious riches, which have been given to us in Christ Jesus.

Since my brother was able to do things that I couldn't, it made me sad and envious. As a little brother I looked up to him and wanted to be strong like him someday.

Every night after dinner, my dad would lay down in his hospital bed after changing his shirt. He required assistance in brushing his teeth in bed. My mom brought a bucket, toothbrush, toothpaste, and would assist him by holding the bucket. He did not want to go upstairs and use the restroom, since it was an inconvenience for him to ask someone to take him upstairs on the lift.

I would go upstairs to take a shower but I needed help. Since I was not strong enough and too weak to stand up for long periods of time, I took a bucket bath. My mom would fill it with warm water and soap, then I would take the cup in my right hand, fill it with water and pour it on my body. It was the only way I could clean myself. I also had to ask my mom to help me get out of the tub after I was done. Once in a while she would let me use my dad's shower which had a bench. That was easier for me because then I could sit down while she cleaned me. Afterwards my mom would read me a bedtime story and soon after I would fall asleep.

Mornings, we got up at 6. When my mom came back upstairs after making tea for my dad, she would help me get dressed.

Yet, the old envy would resurface as I watched my brother get dressed without help. I called him superman because he was so fast in doing everything.

The school bus picked me up at 7 to take me to Sycamore High School, 45 minutes away with two classrooms for children with special needs. Some could not talk, some were confined to a wheelchair, some had speech problems.

High school students were assigned to help those special education kids to get their lunch. I felt scared at first seeing all of those who were all disabled but it made me realize that I was not all alone in the battle I was facing.

All of us were given a tub of assignments that were to be completed for the day.

Mathematics, reading, and writing assignments along with therapy and speech sessions.

The speech therapist offices were down a few hallways. The speech therapist's name was Linda. I was taught how to make proper lip closure when making P, B, and M words. I was also taught how to talk clearly and learn sequence of events and put pictures in order. Every speech therapy session would last one hour.

"Hello Vikram. How are you?" Linda said as I entered her office in my wheelchair.

"Good," I replied. "How are you?

"Very well. Nice to meet you. Today we will be working on putting these pictures in order. Can you try by yourself first? If you need any help then let me know."

I felt confused looking at the four pictures. One with a messy room, one with a clean room, one with a semi clean room, and one with a T-shirt on the bed. I tried my best to put the pictures in order.

"OK, I am done. Did I get them right?"

"No I see one of them out of order." She explained to me where I went wrong and we moved on to the next exercise.

"OK now I am going to put a few pictures in front of you. Say the name of these animals. "Bear, Bird. Now you say them."

"Ver, Vird.... How did I do?"

"We'll keep practicing Vikram. Here is a sticker for all the hard work that you have done today," she said as she put a Snoopy sticker on my shirt. As she pushed me in my wheelchair back to the classroom I felt tired.

After speech therapy I spent half an hour in the classroom before it was time to go to

physical therapy, downstairs in a huge room. There were mats, tables, weights, clay, and balance beams to practice walking.

"Hi my name is Ieasha Barnes. I am one of the physical therapists here and I will be working with you today. I am going to help you get strong again. Let's go over here," she said as she pushed me to the next room where there was a long line on the ground.

"OK Victor, I want you to eventually be able to walk down this line at a good pace. We will practice walking soon. Can you take any steps or walk now?,"

"Very little. I can take only a few steps before I lose my balance."

"OK, well let's go on the mat first and do some leg exercises." She assisted me to the ground. "Now try your best to raise your left leg up and down. I will assist you as well."

I tried but was only able to lift my leg three times. Iesha helped me to raise my leg five extra times. After that we moved on to the table. "OK Vikram squeeze this ball as hard as you can. Try."

I tried to squeeze the ball using my left arm but managed to do it just once. It seemed obvious I did not have much strength in the left side of my body.

Once the therapy session was over, it was back to the classroom to work on my assignments. It was extremely difficult, requiring me to go over the material numerous times before I could say I truly understood and retained the material.

When it was time for lunch, I was assigned to a buddy to help, Alisa, who was patient with me since I moved much slower than other kids.

When we got to the cafeteria, I noticed how big it was. A converted gymnasium with about 12 lunch tables. I walked with her through the long line but my left leg was getting very tired. "Are we almost there? I am getting tired and need to sit down," I said, leaning on my cane.

Alisa offered to bring my food to the table. I picked out one where many of my classmates were sitting.

The kids at the table were nice to me. Some of them were from my classroom, some were not. I wanted to fit in the conversation but all they were talking about was sports. It was hard for me to relate sine I could not play and did not like to watch sports on TV either.

While eating lunch, my mind flashed back to the days in the hospital where the only nourishment I got came via feeding tubes. I thought, life is so much better now. The food was so good, I savored every bite.

One day I tried to play with the tether ball and I fell down really hard on the ground. I was taken to the nurses' office where she bandaged the wound on my arm from the fall.

As the nurse called my parents to let them know about the fall, I started to cry, asking myself, "Where do I fit in?"

ALL BECAUSE OF A DRUNK DRIVER! PLEASE DON'T DRINK AND DRIVE.

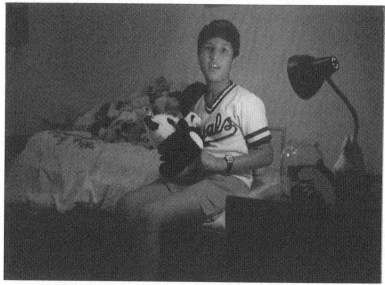

Being left partially paralyzed and with physical limitations I could not run around or play like other kids could, therefore these stuffed animals were considered to be my friends after the crash

Man's best friend! Since I had no friends

Everyone Needs A Friend

That afternoon after getting off the bus, after school my parents were waiting for me, asking how I was doing.

After giving them assurances I was OK, they both gave me a hug, checking my head since they knew I had taken a fall at school.

But my dad sensed all was not right, asking how I was feeling.

"So so I guess."

"Why do you feel like that son?" asked my mom.

"Because I have no friends. I want to have friends like Bicky does. He can run around so much and I just wish I had that kind of life."

"Oh Vikram but just remember our creator God Almighty. He is your friend," my mom said.

"I know but I cannot see him."

"Even though we cannot see him we must always believe that God will and is taking care of us."

Hebrews 11 Faith is the confidence that what we hope for will actually happen; it gives us assurance about things that we cannot see.

"Yes my son. We must always believe,"my dad said.

That did little to lessen my irritation as I went to my room to play with my stuffed animals. They were my friends who I could talk to but they could not respond.

"Hello little Teddy Ruxpin, how are you doing today?"

I turned on the switch so it could talk to me. "Hello my friend. I have a story to tell you today," but it was the same story every day and I knew it by heart so I tried to play with my GI Joes all by myself, in my little bedroom. That got very boring very fast.

As everyone consumed their dinner, I pretended to eat by taking small bites. After everyone finished and were in the family room watching TV, I put the bowl of lentils into the plant next to me.

"Oh WOW son, you finished all of the food that I put in front of you. You are such a good eater," my mom said but soon smelled the lentils coming from the flower pot and looked at me with great disappointment.

"Son what have you done? The food that I give you is supposed to make you strong. It is supposed to give you strength. So please try it next time."

"It taste so bad mommy. I don't like it."

"Some things in life don't taste good but we still have to eat them."

"Yes," my father said. "Look at what I have every day at lunch time. I have two servings of fruit. It's not because I like it but just to keep me strong and healthy for a long life!"

"If I eat all of the fruits, vegetables, and dinner that is given to me will I be able to walk straight again daddy?"

Silence filled the room and then he said, "Well it will help you to walk better my son."

I thought to myself, "Oh boy, the more good food that I eat the better I will be able to do everything. I will be able to use my left hand and leg to full use and be just like everyone else."

That night, I dreamed of walking straight for miles and miles with my family cheering me on. It felt so good to have those kind of dreams. I even had a whole bunch of friends walking with me. Alas, I soon realized, it really was just a dream.

At that time, my brother had a friend, Chad, who would call to make sure he was ready for school and then the two of them would ride their bikes to school together. That did not escape my attention.

"Where's my friend? I need friends too," I complained.

"You have friends at school," my mom said, giving me a big hug.

"It's not the same. They cannot run around like Bicky's friends can. They do not even live close by."

At that point, my parents thought that it might be a good idea if they could hire a baby sitter to play with me, someone who I could be close to and call my friend. The first person they found did not work out. Shelby lasted about three weeks. She ended up playing with my brother half of the time and I did not care for her because she got bored playing with me.

The second girl, whose name was Sally, did not like to play with me as well. She started to play with my brother a lot and did not like playing with me. She lasted for only four weeks. It was not a good fit or match.

The third time was a charm. His name was Shane. He tried to teach me how to ride a bicycle that had training wheels, tried to teach me how to swim and was a very good friend to me. He was able to help my parents out as well. When all of us went on trips to California to look for a house, he went with us to help my mom out. He was the closest person who I could call a friend who would play with me three times a week.

Occasionally, my mom would drive me to classmates who also had physical challenges. Some were unable to walk, speak or eat independently. Most were unable to do all of these things due to a birth defect. One of my classmates, Rosanne, was confined to a wheelchair, unable to eat or speak. She had been that way since birth.

"See," my mom said, "that is why we must give thanks to God Almighty for everything that he has given us. Look at Rosanne. She cannot even do as much as you. Look at how some people have to suffer."

"I know mom but please don't compare me with anybody else. Doesn't everyone want to have the best life? I want to be able to do so many things. Rosanne wants to as well".

"At least you and her can give each other support Vikram."

As we went home I started to feel lonely and wanted to escape from the life that I was living.

Yet, I was still lonely and wanted to escape this life. What is life without a friend? It seemed as if the only friends were the stuffed animals or toys in my room. I could talk to them but they could not respond to me. All of my stuffed animals were the only friends I had besides my babysitter, who would come to play with me twice a week, who we had to pay. I tried to make the best out of my life. Whether I was alone, or with someone, my dad always reminded me over and over that God is your best friend. He is there for you at all times. Turn to him for support.

Exploring Sea World San Diego. We loved Sea World!

All of us ready to leave Kansas City Missouri to leave for San Diego CA. A move we did not want but had to make

During one of our many trips to San Diego CA to look for a house. My babysitter accompanied us to help out

My family and I on a harbor cruise in San Diego CA! We loved bay cruises

Sadly Moving On

While we greatly enjoyed living in Kansas City, with great neighbors, we had no choice but to move.

The situation with my dad forced this decision since the house was three stories, making it difficult for him to get from one floor to the other.

But the other factor was the weather. It was only comfortable for him during spring, March, April and May. At other times it was either too cold or too hot.

So, the choice was San Diego, an area with nearly ideal temperate conditions.

We really loved and treasured our neighbors in Kansas City. They provided us with so much support, always inviting us to their house, hosting dinner parties, and visiting us at our house. They simply were the best. In addition, my brother made great friendships at school.

Our parent's eyes were filled with tears as we all got ready that morning to catch our flight west.

"Looks like this is the last time you will have to take me up the stairs using the wheelchair lift,"my dad said to my mom.

"Yes I know Jasbir. At least in the house in California will be single level. Sorry about all of my frustration Gary. I love to help you. It's just that I get very tired sometimes."

"Yes I understand. OK so now we are here upstairs."

Soon we were all packed and ready. All of our neighbors came to say good-bye.

"Good-bye Roy and Irene," my parents said, greeting one of the couples.

"We sure have enjoyed all of the times we had together. It is sad that you are leaving," they said as they gave my brother and I a big hug.

I stood there, with the help of my cane, and said goodbye to everyone who came to the front door.

Moments later Jan Brachert came to say goodbye to all of us. She brought handcrafted flowers as a going away gift. Her husband and son were there as well.

"Hi y'all, we sure are going to miss you. You know you are always welcome to stay at our place if y'all want to come visit."

"Thank you," my dad said with tears in his eyes.

After they left, our next-door neighbors Kathy, her husband, and their daughter, came to say their farewells.

"Oh saying goodbye is so hard to do. Take care. Please keep in touch," she said, giving my parents a hug.

"We will," said my mom. "Once we arrive in San Diego we will give you a call. Thank you for being such great neighbors. I just don't know how to say bye."

"Well then, don't say bye, just until we meet again, "Kathy said as she gave my brother and I a hug.

Then, it was time to leave. "Goodbye house," I said as the van backed out of the driveway. It was hard for me to leave all of this behind as I reflected upon the few Christmas and New Years that we had in this great neighborhood.

"Do we have everything Jessie? Did we leave anything behind?" my dad asked.

"Only all of those memories that were made. We will hold on to them forever. Every memory except for the bad memory which was the crash."

As we drove by the crash scene, our parents started to pray.

When the plane took off, I looked down at the place where we loved to be but had to leave. Soon all I could see were the memories in my mind.

When the plane landed, I opened my eyes to new surroundings. I noticed so many palm trees and the most beautiful weather.

While we waited for the passengers to deplane, I became envious, watching young and old, all able to walk so fast and go about their day. We were the ones who were the last family to leave, waiting for help to get my father moved.

Getting off the plane and retrieving our luggage took quite an effort. Three people were needed to get my dad from his seat to the wheelchair. Plus, there were four heavy suitcases my mom had to handle herself.

When we were outside, I was amazed how pretty everything was. Beautiful palm trees, blue skies and tall buildings.

"Wow how pretty is this place!" I said with great excitement.

"It sure is a beautiful day," my dad said.

Our new house was a half-hour away but we couldn't stay there as a family until a specialized bathroom was constructed to allow my dad to use it without help. That would take two weeks. We stayed in a motel, just down the street from our new house.

In the meantime, my uncle who came with us on our trip, would stay at the house and keep an eye on it. My brother and I also stayed at the house with him to just get used to it.

We loved to scream in the house and hear the echo of our voice. My brother and I were a bit naughty as kids sometimes are.

One day my brother and I got this huge balloon that was not inflated and we decided to fill it with water. Our uncle warned us that if it popped it would create a huge mess.

So, of course, even after he warned us, we picked it up but the balloon was so heavy, it fell and broke, water sloshing all over the floor.

My uncle was not very happy, either was my mom.

After bringing towels to mop up the mess, she was justifiably angry and scolded us.

"Oh boys if only I had time, I would tell both of you how ashamed I am right now.

Unfortunately, I must go back to the hotel as your dad is all alone. OK I will talk to both of you tomorrow. Now here are the towels."

The next morning, with the floor clean and dry, my brother and uncle were talking about all of the places to see in San Diego, making a list of where to go.

"Victor.... any place that you would like to go to today?" they asked.

"How about to the zoo. I want to go see all of the animals."

"OK let's see what your parents want to do."

After eating breakfast and getting my father ready, we went back to the house and met our next door neighbor, Donald, who brought over a basket of fruit as a Welcome-to the-Neighborhood gift.

We thanked him and asked him about seeing or doing things in San Diego. He suggested the zoo, Sea World and the museums at Balboa Park along with other numerous beaches.

As we got acquainted with our neighbors, the better we felt about our neighborhood. It wasn't as friendly as Kansas City since our neighbors there would visit one another more frequently. In California our neighbors just said hi and bye from the street. My brother hung out a lot with Donald and with a few kids from the neighborhood. I struggled to make friends because I was unable to do many of the activities my brother could do. I was still using the brace on my left arm and leg for support. Simple activities such as riding a skateboard, running or riding a bike were challenging for me.

As hard as everything was I was determined to be just like everyone else. I did not want to have any physical limitations. I strived everyday to learn how to walk straight, run, and be like other kids of my age.

Soon the furniture was delivered and all was well except for the things my dad needed to live independently. An extra bathroom was being constructed and wheelchair ramps were getting installed.

"Oh my son look at all of these hassles that I have to go through just to live an independent life. As for now someone will have to help me go to the bathroom as the door to the other bathrooms are too small for my wheelchair to get into. Sometimes I just feel like giving up....

But then again I say to you son please don't give up on anything that stands in your way in life because God Almighty is always taking care of us.

Philippians 4:13 I can do everything through Christ, who gives me strength.

5th grade and always smiling. No one could take that smile away from me.

School Days

While the move to San Diego was very exciting to everyone, including me, it was an entirely different story when I began school. In Kansas City, I had never really felt overt discrimination due to my disability.

That wasn't the case when I started school in San Diego just a month before my ninth birthday. I lasted only one month in the first school I was enrolled in, thanks to constant harassment and verbal abuse.

There were no other students with disabilities, which made me a target. The comments to, and about me, were incredibly hurtful. The first month seemed to last forever, until I complained enough to my parents, who understood my frustration and enrolled me in a bigger school.

That wasn't much better. Some of the kids would walk past me and call me retarded and other hurtful names.

In the classroom, I was unable to keep up the pace with the other students, unable to remember the information and so I was placed in special education.

I remember one particular exchange I had when some of the kids noticed I was limping and had the brace and cane.

"Hi, what's your name?" they asked.

"Hi, my name is Victor. I am new to this school."

"Hey why do you have that brace on your left leg for and why do you have that arm brace on for?"

"I was involved in a car crash," I replied.

"Well you look like a retard limpy. Can we call you limpy?", they said, then tried to make me fall by taking my cane away from me.

"Hey I need that for support," I pleaded with them, "I can't walk without it. Please give it back to me."

Finally, a teacher came out of her classroom and got the cane back for me.

"Shame on everyone for picking on this sweet, innocent child. Now say your sorry and apologize."

While they said they were sorry, I wasn't so sure. I just hoped it would never happen again. After the incident, I was introduced to my special education teacher, Mrs. Mason, who explained she would test me in math, reading and comprehension to accurately gauge what level I had reached.

She gave me a few written and verbal tests and I was then given assignments to work on. Some were easy, some were hard. Everyday I was given a reading assignment, helped by a teacher's assistant who read with me.

Often, I would start to laugh while reading as I had no control over the laughter. The teachers could not understand why I would start to laugh and neither did I. It was like as if I had no control over anything. I was helpless not knowing what do to. All I knew was that all I could do was the best that I could do and leave the rest up to God Almighty.

Psalm 3:5 Trust in the LORD with all your heart; do not depend on your own understanding. Seek his will in all you do, and he will show you which path to take.

When Life Takes Another Dive

I graduated from elementary school in 1990 and was looking forward to junior high. I had mixed feelings, though. On one hand, I was anticipating going forward but was somewhat sad to leaving the staff and friends I made.

That summer, we had a major scare. My dad was complaining about severe pain in his stomach. At times, the pain was so bad he would lose his breath. We were scared and hoped it would pass but the pain increased in severity. We called the ambulance to take him to the hospital.

As the doctors began the tests, we waited patiently for the results. I remember my dad once telling me, "Health is wealth. If you have your health you have everything." Now that my dad's health was getting worse I understood this even more than before.

"OK," the doctor said, "we cannot exactly pinpoint the problem or make a diagnosis at this time but we do know that there is a lot of gas that he is unable to release. So we are going to keep him in the hospital to run some more tests and send him home in a few days when we know what the exact problem is."

"Thank you doctor. I do not like to see him in so much pain," my mom said.

"Well everything will be OK. We are going to find out what the exact problem is. Don't worry Mrs. Grewal. Everything is going to be OK."

When we all went home that evening, it felt strange not to have my dad there. My dad and I formed a strong bond, supporting each other through our disabilities. We visited as often as we could.

"Oh son, at first I thought life was hard and all I wanted to do was walk again. However, now life has presented me with more complex problems and now all I ask God for is to take away this pain in my stomach. Not being able to walk was one problem but now this pain in my stomach is an even bigger problem. It hurts so bad. I feel so bad, having to be a burden to all of you."

"Don't worry Gary, you are not being a burden to any one of us. We are here to help you. Isn't that what family is for? To help one another out in time of need," my mom said.

The doctor prescribed five different prescriptions, my dad would have to take several times throughout the day. Without them, my dad would not be able to get out of bed or do anything.

Now, instead of getting ready in an hour or two, it took much longer. Every waking hour, he was taking medication, starting when he awoke at 7:30. He would have his tea with my mom, then watch TV for about half an hour.

Then, it was transfer to the wheelchair to go to the bathroom. Shave, transfer to the toilet, back to the wheelchair, transfer to the shower, dry off, back to the wheelchair and then back to bed.

Once in bed, he would exercise for an hour, catheterize, have his breakfast, and then get dressed.

What once took maybe two hours, now had almost doubled.

The medication could only help for a certain amount of time. He could not be up past 6 or 7 because that is when the medication had worn off by that and his stomach would be hurting again. Laying down reduced the spasms and was also restricted in the foods that he could eat. His diet consisted of mostly cereal without milk, fruit, bread, eggs, and lentils. It was a hard lifestyle for him to get used to.

"Oh Victor what ever happened to the life I once had. Everything changed in a blink of an eye. Oh how I wish I could be able to get ready fast like I used to or eat the foods that I love to eat. This life has become too hard for me to live," he wept from time to time.

Psalm 119:50 Your promise revives me; it comforts me in all my troubles.

"Hold on dad please don't give up. We must have courage. Just like you always tell me to never give up, now I am going to try to encourage you as well."

Joshua 1:9 This is my command be strong and courageous! Do not be afraid or discouraged. For the LORD your God is with you wherever you go.

"I know, my son, thank you for that reminder. I will try," he replied with tears in his eyes.

As an outlet to relax and take my mind off of my disability I often turned to music to escape. Music was and still is my everything.

Music Is My Everything

Music has been a huge part of my life as long as I can remember. I listened to the radio and also nagged my parents to buy me records and tapes and liked just about every kind of music except classical.

Early on, I was introduced to the great music of Whitney Houston, The Go-Go's and Toni Basil. I loved the song. "When The Children Cry" by White Lion. The lyrics struck a strong chord in me, and I did not feel all alone. The drunk driver left me crying and helpless as a child. As the lyrics say 'Little child dry your crying eyes.' As a child was always crying as I could not understand what was happening to me or why I was going through so much misery.

Cyndi Lauper's "Change of Heart" was another one of my favorites. I thought of how life would someday have a change of heart and set me free from my disability. In the later years when I was in college, the song by MC Lyte called "Keep on.... Keep on" inspired me to keep going for the certificate I was working on despite of all of the negative comments I got from my professor.

The song by Lisa Fischer,"How Do I Ease The Pain" was a very healing song to my heart of times when a girl who I liked at school would go with someone else.

"Toy Soldiers" by Martika made me feel as if I could get right back up even when I fell. Somehow music pushed me to do more in life despite of my permanent injuries.

My parents were very picky in what kind of music that they let my brother and I listen to. The music could have no sex or violence in it and many times it was hard to find music that they would let us listen to. Michael Jackson was one of my favorites. I listened to the album over and over again. Madonna was another one of my favorites.

Jackson's "Man In The Mirror" helped me to strive to be the best person that I could be. "Live To Tell" by Madonna, made me think how hard but great it would be if I could live to tell the story of how a drunk driver changed my life forever, which I have done.

When I was in the tenth grade, I heard the song by The Shamen called "Move Any Mountain." When I heard it, I felt I could do anything and that nothing would stand in my way. The song "I've Got The Power" from Snap, made me feel powerful and strong, like I could do anything.

Sometimes, the rhythm of the music inspired me to do more than I was capable of. Music had such an influence I even started to save my lunch money and buy cassette tapes instead of eating. I used to run down the street from my school to buy music without my parents even knowing. It knew it was dangerous at times but it was the only way that I could get the music I loved.

One day after school I ran to the music store which was about a mile away. On my way back a woman offered to give me a ride back to school. I was very scared but she was insistent. I remembered what I had learned in school and from my parents about never taking rides from strangers. I don't know how or why but I ended up in the car with her.

Her name was Peggy and she was prepared with questions, where did I want to be dropped off? What happened to me? What was my name?

She dropped me off at school, and said, "I work with a lot of people with disabilities in my profession. I'm a speech and language pathologist. I will pray for you and that The good Almighty Lord heal to heal you. Be strong. Jesus loves you."

I then made a promise to myself I would never take a ride from anyone I did not know.

One week later. I just had to have Keith Sweat's song that seemingly played a million times a day, "I'll Give All My Love To You" so I started walking from my house to the music store, about a mile away. I was doing so good and was almost there when a motorcycle cop pulled over.

"Hi Kid how are you?"

"I am OK," I responded hesitantly.

"No need to be afraid. I noticed you are walking with a limp. Is everything OK. Are you hurt?"

"Yes everything is OK," I replied, just wanting to walk away and get my music.

"Are you supposed to be in school?"

"No we had half a day at school today. School is over for the day."

"What school do you go to?"

"The local Junior High School right up the street from here."

"OK, well I am going to take you home now. It is not safe for you to be walking around all alone."

"I'm not going home on the back of that motorbike. I am afraid that I will fall off."

"Nothing will happen," the cop reassured me.

"No I want to be in a police car."

He then called for a police car to come pick me up.

I waited with him for about half an hour but his questions about my disability made me uncomfortable bringing back upleasant memories I hated. It tore me up, having to deal with all of the emotions that go along with a life that has been turned upside down! I often turned to God Almighty in times like these and found my peace in life.

Galations 6:09 So let's not get tired of doing what is good. At just the right time we will reap a harvest of blessing if we do not give up.

Soon the police car arrived and I was placed in the back seat. I thought it was kind of cool to have been taken home and directed the policeman to my house. When we arrived, the policeman explained to my parents what had happened. My parents were upset.

"Do you know what could have happened Victor? You could have fallen down and gotten hurt," my mom said in a stern voice.

"Victor, never leave the house ever again without telling us where you are going! We are responsible for your safety," my dad said to me.

I thought to myself, "All I want is that music but these limitations prevent me from going to the store to buy what I want and need."

My brother helped me tremendously to buy some music every week. He would go to the store on his bicycle and buy me all of the music I requested. I was very happy but envied him. He knew how to ride a bike but I never could ride a bike independently after the crash.

It was hard for me to adjust to all of the limitations that life had presented me with.

Music played a huge role to keep me motivated, to help me overcome my disability in order to do every-day activities. It pushed me beyond my limitations and nothing or no one would stop me! Music was, and still today remains, my everything. For me living without music is impossible.

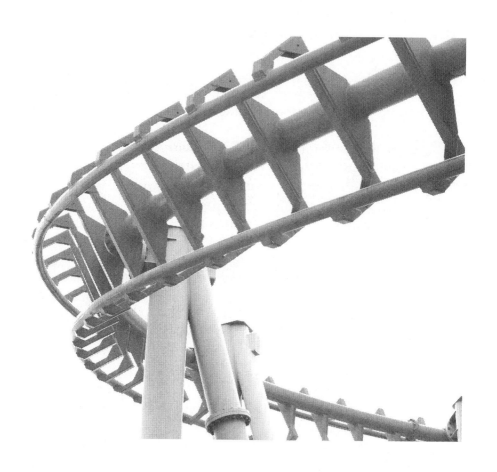

Junior High School

As my elementary school years passed by very fast 7th grade was approaching. I felt sad leaving the elementary school. I was leaving so many teachers behind who I thought were really great! All of the teachers and principal at the school were so nice to me. I considered them as my friends. They understood my disability and were understanding of my strengths and weaknesses. I cried at my elementary school graduation as I did not like to move on. One of the things I hated in life was change and how everything changes. My parents always taught me that the one thing that will never change is God's love for you. Lamentations 3:22-23 The faithful love of the LORD never ends! His mercies never cease. Great is his faithfulness; his mercies begin afresh each morning.

I felt nervous moving on to a bigger school but knew that eventually I would get used to it, with a lot more students. In the back of my head I always was thinking if people could relate to me and how they would treat me since I walk differently.

After a well rested summer August quickly approached and 7th grade orientation was coming up. As my mom drove me to school and dropped me off I slowly walked over to where the other students were standing.

"Oh hi Victor are you ready for seventh grade? We are finally here. Can you believe how fast elementary school passed us by. Now it is the big 7", my friend that I made from elementary school said to me.

"Yes I know. I am ready, I guess", I replied.

"OK let's go over to get our picture taken for our class ID cards. Come on and we'll walk together."

I was grateful for her friendship as she always seemed to have so much patience to wait for me. It always took me more time to get to my destination than other kids. I was a great runner though. I was always able to run better and fast than I could walk. I did not understand why, Doctors did not even know why.

Orientation was fun. They even had a DJ and food. I was a dancing machine back in Junior High School. I loved music and I loved to dance. I was actually able to build up the strength in my left leg by dancing.

The first day of school was challenging since it was a new campus and all of my classrooms were spread about. I was placed in special education for almost every subject. I found special education to be too easy for me. I hated special education PE. I had to go to another school for the first period which was PE. The teacher I had would not even let me run the track. Instead I rode a stationary bicycle for the entire time of the PE session. The other students in my class were allowed to run the track and do exercises that the teacher would restrict me from doing. He thought I would get hurt if I were to run or do push ups. It made me very frustrated. After PE I would go back to one Junior High School from another Junior High School. After I would go to special education English, Math, and would have one Speech session where I would work with the speech and language pathologist in making proper lip closure when speaking.

I did not like special education as it was just not for me. The reason why I was placed in these classes was because of my short term memory deficit. There were other students who had behavioral issues which I didn't have much of. The only behavior problem I had was that I would laugh at irregular times which I could not control.

"Mom, dad, I am so tired of school as it is way too easy for me. I need more challenging work. They are limiting me too much in what I can and cannot do. Please help me!" My parents could see how tenacious I was and how much I wanted to excel in my studies.

I told the teachers as well. They set up a parent teacher conference. I had no idea as to why I have a voice, I often thought to myself. Is anyone listening to me? Where do I fit in? All I know is all of this education is way too easy for me and something has got to change or else I would go crazy.

The following day as I waited for the bus I thought about all that I could do in life and how nothing would stand in my way. Not education, physical activities, nor the comments that people would make, or anything. I felt like I could break all boundaries and have no limitations. This would be hard but with my faith in God Almighty I would be able to get through this.

Philippians 4:13 For I can do everything through Christ who gives me strength.

I started to try to walk as straight as I could which was only 5 steps at a time. This was not easy for me and something that I could not do without concentrating. Something that helped me a lot to walk straight was music and a beat that kept me going.

My teacher held a parent teacher conference meeting that I was allowed to attend. In the meeting was my special education teacher and my parents.

"Hello Mr. and Mrs. Grewal how are you doing today?"

"We are doing good. Thank you very much. How are you doing Mrs. Orr?"

(Cut through all of the greetings let's get down to business) I thought in the back of my mind.

"How are you doing Victor," my teacher Mrs. Orr asked me.

"I am doing good. Can we please get to the point of this meeting here!"

OK so you want to be placed in mainstream classes rather than special education classes. Is that correct?"

"Well I would like the work to be more challenging and I would like for there not to be so many interruptions by other students who are misbehaving. I want to learn. I am also tired of going to the other Jr. High School for special education PE. I am not being challenged enough in that PE session. I can do a lot more."

"Now son," my dad started to say, "Is that really what you want? Don't you think that then it would be too challenging?"

"I want to be challenged. I am tired of this easy homework and easy classes. I want to be more challenged. I want to be just like everybody else," I responded and shed a tear.

"Yes Victor your dad is right. Think about this and what you want to do. In the regular education classes the work is more challenging and they go at an accelerated pace," Mrs. Orr said.

"Yes son please think about it," my mom said.

"OK I have thought about it and my answer is that I want out of special education classes and into regular education," I replied.

"For all of the subjects. Math, English, and PE? That may be hard for you to handle all at once," my teacher said to me.

"OK we will talk to our son more about this at home," my parents said as the meeting came to an end.

As we all left the meeting my dad said to me, "Oh my son people in your and my shoes must be more understanding of others and accept life for the way it is." As he said these words I sat with my chin down in great sadness.

Matthew 5:4 Blessed are they that mourn: for they shall be comforted.

"Victor, son, you heard what your teacher said. Give yourself and her a week to think about the move that you want to make and then we'll see what will happen. Your mom and I are by your side and support you."

"Then why do I feel all alone Dad?"

"How do you feel all alone Son? God is with you. Remember that."

"I know but with my disability. Why must it be so hard to get what I want? I feel as if no one at school can relate to me either. All the kids in my class have behavioral problems. I just want to be like everyone else. Will there ever be a cure for my disability?"

"Someday there will be, I promise you son. Until then we must not lose heart and keep going so that we can be strong."

I kept my father's voice inside my mind and the constant reminder that someday there would be a cure. That was and is my hope.

The next day as I got ready to go to school I was hoping that it would be a good day and that no one would make fun of me. I was hoping that my day would go smoothly. I put on my clothes, had a good breakfast, and ran up the street to catch the bus. As I got to school and had a seat outside the classrooms on the benches next to all of the classmates at school along came a group of kids.

"Hi Victor. Is that your name?"

"Yes it is," I replied. "How are you? I see you guys on campus a lot. I just did not have the opportunity to meet you."

"Hi my name is Alajandro and these are my friends Chris and Doug. Hey we were wondering if you are part of a gang. Your left hand makes all these weird movements and gang signs. Are those gang signs? What does this sign mean that you make with your left hand," they looked at me laughing as they walked away making me feel really bad.

"Don't pay any attention to those kids," Alisha another student said to me. "I look up to you and how brave you are. It must not be easy to do all the things that you do but you are making the best out of every circumstance."

"Thank you Alisha. I appreciate that so much."

I looked down at my left hand feeling totally sad and tried to control the movements I made with my left hand. Be courageous I said to myself. I won't let their words get me down. I always felt like I had a shield in front of me to protect me from all of these hurtful words that people would say to me. That shield was God Almighty. He would save me from times like these. At least there were kind people like Alisha to say nice words to me when others would put me down. These people were like angels. I felt very happy that at least they were there to encourage me and to smile or to say a nice word to me.

I also slowly made other friends or people who did not put me down or make fun of my disability. Sometimes the kids who were nice to me had friends who were not nice to me.

That was very hard for me, I had to separate myself from the people who were nice to me because their friends were not. The big question for me at this time in my life was where do I exactly fit in?

ALL BECAUSE OF A DRUNK DRIVER! PLEASE DON'T DRINK AND DRIVE

S is for Suicide

They say time heals all wounds but that certainly wasn't true for me. Some nine years after the crash was still vivid in my mind.

It was at this moment of my life that I contemplated suicide.

There was the pain of constantly hearing hurtful, mean words thrown my way and, bad as that was, there was something else that cut even deeper.

I had come to the bitter realization that at 14 years of age, the life that I envisioned for myself couldn't materialize.

The song from Rocky 4 played in my mind. Survivor's lyrics, "There's no easy way out. There's no short cut home. Giving in can't be wrong" were the lyrics that played in my mind 1,000 times a day.

Enveloped in sadness, I turned to my parents.

"Son, don't give up," my dad pleaded. "Please don't give up. I am here for you and God Almighty is here for you."

"I know, but life is too hard for me to live. All of these people saying harmful and hurtful words to me. They call me retard right to my face. It feels awful," I said, and started to cry. "What should I do dad? Can you please tell me what I should do? I am tired of trying to find answers."

"Well my son the only thing we can do is turn to God Almighty in times like these. Now let's close our eyes, fold our hands and pray and ask for God's help through this very trying time." As I closed my eyes he led me in a prayer.

After the prayer, I asked, "OK, so now what dad?"

"Now we must have courage and continue to live life in accordance to the way God has taught us to live. Please don't feel hopeless because God has given you a lot. Never give up. Can you please promise me that?"

"OK I will try," I replied.

"Remember God has a plan. God wants you to love the life he has given you. It will break my heart and your mom's heart if you were found dead and committed suicide."

My mom had been shopping and when she came into the kitchen, immediately sensed something was wrong.

"He is very sad," my dad told her. "Life has become very hard for him to endure. He needs encouragement and needs to be uplifted."

"Oh Victor, I wish there were something else I could do than show you my love and support. I love you Victor." As she said those words my brother came running in the house after playing with his friends.

"Hi mom, hi dad, Hi Vict..., wait, what's wrong?"

With my face drenched with tears, I looked at him with envy. He leaned forward with open arms to give me a hug. As I hugged him back, I was shaking in fear.

"You have everything. I have nothing. I wish I were like you," I said mournfully.

"You will be.... You just have to wait," he replied.

"How much longer do I have to wait? It's already been too long of a wait. I can't wait any longer."

"Oh son, please calm down. Everything is going to be OK," my dad said.

I soon calmed down but the thoughts of suicide never completely escaped my consciousness.

At times I felt like a soldier who kept getting knocked down with words and insults but still continued to march ahead. It was not easy but something I had to to do, to be strong,

courageous, and keep on moving ahead even when life was not fair. It was not easy. Every time I felt like giving up, I always remembered my father's words "My son please never give up."

God and my family kept me holding on to life and never ever giving up. They were there to listen and give me love.

But honestly, while I had my family's support along with the friends I made at school, I still felt isolated.

To mentally escape my pain, I turned to reading. Fictional books allowed my mind to enter into someone else's life, to escape reality as it was a constant struggle to keep my hands away from that knife drawer in the kitchen or the floor cleaner.

There were times my mind would be crying out, "Mercy, mercy. I can't take it anymore! Please God take me home. All I want to do is be with you. Far away from all the people who call me hurtful names, far away from all the people who do not understand my needs. I don't want to be me anymore. I want to be someone else."

I tried to imitate people as to how they would walk, talk, and behave. I tried the hardest I

could to walk straight for as long as I could. Sometimes, I used to snap my fingers so as I could walk to the rhythm of my snapping fingers. All I wanted to do was fit in with everyone else.

ALL BECAUSE OF A DRUNK DRIVER! PLEASE DON'T DRINK AND DRIVE

High School Years

I have mentioned this before, but I repeat—I hated change.

Yet, change is inevitable. I graduated from junior high school to 10th grade, and that made me uncomfortable.

At first, I was so lonely, I kept going back to my old junior high school at lunchtime to visit friends I missed.

But eventually I adjusted. I reconnected with friends from junior high who were already in high school. And except a very few, most of my classmates accepted me for who I was.

I was placed into special education classes in English, math, and science. I tried it but soon realized that it was not my cup of tea and I wanted regular education classes instead.

The biggest complaint I had was the same problem I encountered in junior high. There were so many disciplinary incidents, I wasn't learning much since the teachers focused on maintaining order in the classroom rather than actual teaching.

I felt stuck, making a request to the teacher, my counselor and my parents that I be allowed to move into regular education classes. In order to make this happen my parents had to have a conference with my teachers and discuss it, just like I did when I was in the seventh grade.

When I got into the 11th grade, I was placed in regular education English 10. I was nervous, at first, being a year older than the rest of my classmates and it was hard for me to keep up. This was the only mainstream class that I took and homework for this class took me seven hours to complete but I did it to prove that I could do anything. I just wanted to be like other students so I pushed myself.

I didn't get very much sleep as my studies were so intense. At times I thought this was an advanced placement class because it was so tough.

"Oh son, we are so proud of you," my mom said as I was doing my homework late one night. "You are working very hard to complete this course."

"Yes, well I am trying to. It is hard. Spending all of these long hours trying to complete all of these assignments. I just want to be like everyone else. That is my dream and to be accepted into the University of my choice."

"Oh son, you are very ambitious, I commend you on that," my dad said to me.

"Thank you dad, for all your love and support. I know I can do anything if I put my mind to it," I replied feeling grateful.

"You're welcome my son that's what fathers are for."

At this point, seeing how I had matured, my dad asked me to start making him the tea he so loved, in the morning and at night, instructing me how to make it.

First he told me to fill the pan with water, then put the stove on and let the water come to a boil, then put a tea bag in the water and wait for five minutes. Afterwards I put a little bit milk in the tea. He wasn't allowed sugar so we used an Equal Sweetener in the tea.

I did this twice a day, morning and evening. My mom also made the tea from time to time when I was too rushed and did not have time to make it.

Between making tea for my dad and working late into the night to complete my homework, it was an exhausting time for me.

I had to be dressed and ready to go by 6:45 a.m. when the school bus would come to my driveway to pick me up. The bus was full of kids with disabilities, with different levels of severity. One girl was blind, one was unable to walk, talk, or even feed herself and one of the kids was mentally disabled. We each had our own unique disability and struggles to deal with.

I made friends at school with the students who did not have disabilities and felt like a

"wannabe". I wanted to walk like everyone else, be in the same level of education and act the same way as they were. I wanted to escape the reality of my disability.

I even took the SAT's and applied to the University of California, Santa Barbara in my senior year. My parents supported me the whole way through.

"Tomorrow I take my SAT so I can go to UCSB and study to become a librarian," I announced.

"Good luck my son. You will do great. Have you been studying those SAT books that we bought for you?" asked my dad.

"Oh yes. I have and I remember the formula for pi is 3.14. I hope I will be able to pass this test with top scores."

"Say a prayer before going to do your test. God will help you get through all of the tough questions," my dad answered.

But in the back of my mind, something kept telling me that I would not be able to score high on this test and get into the university of my choice. I knew my level of math and English was not at college level. I was placed in regular education English twelve and regular education basic math when I got in the 12th grade. I did not even know how to do algebra, geometry, or calculus and I was taking this basic math class so I could pass the exit exam in high school.

I could not even pass the math section of these exams. I was however able to pass the other two exams by the skin of my teeth which I was grateful for. I was able to graduate high school because I was in special education and did not want to leave all of the people who helped me and all of the friends I would be leaving behind.

College Years

Following high school graduation, I had the naive notion that college would be easier.

But the idea quickly evaporated.

I enrolled in the local community college near my house, signing up for classes in pre-algebra, English College Writing 1, and Art 100. Some of my former high school classmates were already in the advanced classes of math and English. I knew I was a bit behind in my studies but I thought to myself: I'd always be two steps behind. Everything in my life takes me double or triple the time to complete.

As I walked into the Pre-Algebra class I felt nervous. Sitting with a huge text book right in front of me and a binder that was full of papers that would soon be filled to capacity. As the class got in session the professor walked in and explained what would be covered: fractions, decimals, equations, and how to calculate the circumference of a circle and odd shapes.

As she explained the material, I tried to act as if it would be no big deal. Everything in the first half of class was similar to the material taught to me in high school.

Testing always made me nervous. While the classroom was silent, I would start to laugh. It was embarrassing since I had no control over the urge to laugh even when it was inappropriate. Eventually, I would take my tests in the tutoring center. I would be nervous there as well but at least I would not have many people around me.

I received a C on my first pre-algebra test. It was easy, just a review of addition, subtraction, multiplication and division. I could have done better if only I hadn't rushed through it. Oh well, I thought to myself, I will do better.

It had been over a dozen years since the crash and, as much as I tried to forget, there were constant reminders of that night.

It was still difficult to get around physically but that was a minor inconvenience compared to my short-term memory deficit, that had been a problem all through school and it became an even bigger barrier as I attended college. I was unable to retain even after hours and hours of studying. It was very frustrating.

"Victor, how are you doing?" the professor asked me after I received a D on my third exam in the class.

"I am doing good. This information that you are teaching us is way too fast for me to grasp."

"Well, you do look a little bit nervous when I see you in class. I just hope, are you comfortable with everything?"

"Yes I am."

"You know, there is tutoring available in the library. You should use it. It is free to all students who attend this college and will help you."

I explained to her my difficulty in retaining information.

She responded: "You know, if you do continue to have great difficulty in this class and get low marks on your exams you may want to consider dropping this class as your GPA will not get affected. You can always sign up again and take it at a later time."

My dad even hired a tutor to come to the house and help me. Even that did not help. "How am I going to go to the university if I can not even pass this math class?" I asked him "This information is just too hard to remember. It just gets so frustrating and discouraging living with a brain injury I can't do anything about. All I want is to go to the university to earn a masters in library science."

Isaiah 58:11 The LORD will guide you continually, giving you water when you are dry and restoring your strength. You will be like a well watered garden, like an ever flowing spring.

As for English, at first, I thought it would be easy, since I loved to read and write but it became much too hard, I tried to pass it three times but eventually dropped out. Art was also difficult but I finally managed to pass with a C.

After failed attempts to pass the pre-algebra or English, I decided to look into certificate programs, thinking that would be an easier route to getting to a career working in a library. I enrolled in a couple of library science courses at the college and passed with an A and a B.

The first class was to introduce all of the different resources the library has. I was given a workbook and was to find information in different resources in the library. In the second class, the primary assignment was to make a thesis statement, then find 10 reliable sources of information to back it up. My thesis: cartoons lead kids to violence. I used books, magazines, newspaper and other resources to find information as evidence and I received a B in this class.

After the completion of these courses at Mira Costa College, I searched various websites of colleges in San Diego. I finally found a certificate program at a community college that was half an hour from my house. It offered a certificate in library technology courses and I thought that this would be the perfect field of study for me. It would be a job that would not be very physically challenging. But what really attracted me to this job the most was my love for reading and literature.

I enrolled in the library technician program at Palomar College in San Marcos, taking the most basic course introduction to libraries and information science. I took one course at a time so I wouldn't get overwhelmed with information. There were six library technology courses and four other required courses in accounting, English, computers, filing, and a business class.

While I worked diligently throughout the two years it took me to complete the certificate program I also volunteered at a local library two nights a week. I did this to get exposure to the library and so that it would look good on my resume. I also thought that I might have a chance at getting hired at this library once a position opened up.

I went in to interview for the volunteer position, explaining I was currently in the library technology certificate program and was hoping to get exposure to library work. The librarian told me what my duties would be, including shelving books, emptying the book drops, and learning the Dewey Decimal system.

As I drove home that night, I truly felt I was on a career path that God had chosen for me. Week after week I continued to put one hundred percent of my energy into my volunteer work. It took me a while to remember how to shelve books by author especially if it was the same author of a book but a different title. I eventually got the grasp of everything and I enjoyed it.

While volunteer work was great I also needed a paying job so in the summer of 1998, I found my first paying job working at the amusement park in Carlsbad. I was hired at a seasonal summer job fair. It was a great accomplishment for me. I was a refreshment stand employee.

The supervisor explained my responsibilities, to pick up buckets of ice as well as cleaning dishes from tables. She then asked if I could do this, a query that always irked me. I hated it when asked if I could do specific jobs. If I couldn't, I would ask for help.

Everyday, I was lifting the buckets of ice to put in the soft drink machines, getting the place ready to open by 9 a.m., picking up the dishes from the tables after guests were done eating, putting them in the dish room, and sweeping the floors. I did a great job and my boss was very pleased with all of the work I was doing.

"Victor....can I talk to you for a minute?"

"Sure, is there anything wrong?"

"No not at all, I just want to let you know that we are going to move you to another place to work. I think that would be more safe for you. It makes me nervous when you walk and hold trays. I keep thinking that you are going to drop one of those trays. It will be much safer for you to as well because I am scared that you will fall down in the dish room every time you enter.

"Nothing has happened so far. I have been safe," I replied, feeling sad that she doesn't want me to work there anymore just because of my disability.

That assignment was The Burger Stop. After Penny introduced me to my new supervisor Sherry, I never bothered to say goodbye.

I was very well respected at The Burger Stop. I worked in the kitchen and was also expected to keep the grounds clean where the guests ate. I did everything expected of me and earned an award for doing such a superior job. I was even given compliments by guests of how much they loved to see my big smile.

Struggling To Achieve

Words were my salvation... but at times different words hurt as much as a physical blow to my body.

I was inspired during this time by "When You Believe" by Whitney Houston and Mariah Carey.

Oh yes, there can be miracles when you believe.

Though hope is frail,

It's hard to kill.

Who knows what miracles You can achieve When you believe somehow you will You will when you believe.

They don't always happen when you ask And it's easy to give into your fears.

But when you are blinded by your pain Can't see your way safe through the rain Thought of a still resilient voice, says love is very near."

I played that song in my car whenever I felt discouraged and needed that extra push to keep me going and told myself no matter what happens, I would keep going towards my dream and goal of working in the library as a library technician.

Psalm 55:16-17 As for me, I call to God and the LORD saves me. Evening, morning and noon, I cry out in my distress, and he hears my voice.

Conversely, my dreams nearly shattered by an unfailing professor who bluntly told me I would never get a job in the library.

Those words stung, but my reply was equally blunt and to the point.

"That's your opinion. You'll see I will be able to pass this class and will get a job in the library." And with that, I got up and left her office feeling hurt and angry by her words. Those words "you will never be able to get a job in the library" haunted me. I tried my hardest to get those words out of my mind.

That evening I asked my dad for advice on what I should I do and how do I ignore the negativity towards me.

"My son, my brave son, there are many things that people will say to you in this world.

Some may try to put you down, some may try to pull your spirits up with a nice word or compliment. We must not depend on what other people say. We must only depend on

God Almighty for support because he is our biggest source of strength in life. Do what your heart tells you to do. I see that you have a love for working in the library. I see you studying very hard to achieve this goal. I see that your heart is set on working as a library technician in the library. Do you want to achieve this goal?"

"Oh yes I do. I want this so bad and know I can do this with the help of God Almighty!"

"OK then just ignore what your professor said to you. Prove her wrong."

Philippians 4:6-7
Don't worry about anything: instead, pray about everything. Tell God what you need, and thank him for all he has done. Then you will experience God's peace, which exceeds anything we can understand. His peace will guard your hearts and minds as you live in Christ Jesus.

A week later I had a brief, unpleasant conversation with my professor.

"Oh, so have you given it any thought of what I told you about employment in the library?" she asked.

"Yes I have, and yes, I do plan to pursue a career and study in this field. Thank you very much for your concern," I said abruptly and walked away.

It was still hard, though, as I struggled to maintain my hold on to the faith that God was going to bring me through this dark time where some were trying to discourage me but I could hear God telling me to hold on. I tried not to have bad feelings towards these people who were trying to discourage me. I felt like as if I carried a shield called Jesus in front of me to protect myself from these words that I did not want to hear. Even though some people tried to discourage me I could always heard God telling me to hold on. At the same time I tried to not have any bad feelings towards these people and tried to turn the other cheek.

Matthew 5:38
You have heard that it was said, "An eye for an eye and a tooth for a tooth. But I say to you, do not resist an evildoer.
But if anyone strikes you on the right cheek, turn the other also."

This verse had become a way of life for me and this is what my dad had taught me from the bible. "This life may not be easy but we must not lose heart and have courage my son. Be brave and depend on God Almighty when discouraged."

While continuing my studies and volunteer work, I visualized myself at the library: processing library materials, assisting patrons in locating library materials, and having my own name badge, Victor S. Grewal County Library Technician.

But now, after all the volunteer work, I was ready for a paying job. I asked the librarian what I needed to do to gain employment here.

She explained I needed to submit an application, and take a test for the position I wanted. "We have a library technician and a library page application. I think you should apply for the library page job," she told me. That would be right up your alley. You've been fulfilling those duties as a volunteer, might as well get paid for it."

In the following weeks, I carefully noted my duties as a volunteer. I was very meticulous about my duties. After putting the books on the cart in order, one of the employees would check the accuracy. I was soon given more responsibilities such as putting the newspapers on the shelves and checking them into the library. I was learning and doing everything I could to prove to everybody that I could do this work.

My dad was a constant source of encouragement.

"Don't worry my son they will notice all of your hard work and offer you a position when the position opens up. If you are doing your best and are good, they will hire you."

Matthew 5:3-10
"Blessed are the poor in spirit, for theirs is the kingdom of heaven.
Blessed are those who mourn, for they will be comforted.
Blessed are the meek, for they will inherit the whole earth.
Blessed are those who hunger and thirst for righteousness, for they will be filled.
Blessed are the merciful, for they will be shown mercy.
Blessed are the pure in heart, for they will see God.
Blessed are the peacemakers, for they will be called the children of God.
Blessed are those who are persecuted because of righteousness, for theirs is the kingdom of heaven.

Patience was a virtue I learned early on. Not only did I have to have patience waiting for the job I desired, but also while in that rehabilitation hospital for seven months before finally getting released. I had to have patience dealing with my short-term memory deficit. I sometimes felt my mind was trapped in a jail cell with no way out, dealing with what life was putting me through, yet it was something I had no control over.

I tried to explore new, bigger, and better opportunities to live a fulfilled life. The song by Soul Asylum called "Runaway Train" tremendously helped me get through these mysterious times in my life as the lyrics resonated in my mind:

It seems no one can help me now.
I'm in too deep there's no way out.
Runaway train never going back
Wrong way on a one way track.
Seems like I should be getting somewhere.
Somehow I am neither here nor there.
Can you help me remember how to smile
Make it all seem worthwhile.
How on earth did I get so jaded?
Life's mysteries seem so faded."

While listening, I did not feel alone and felt strength in the songs I heard on the radio. This was the one song that helped me get through the most difficult days of my life.

One day after, class I was trying to keep up with one of my classmates, Cindy, as she went to her car. She was walking so fast as I could not keep up but I needed to ask her a question about the homework that was due for the next class session.

"Cindy can I ask you something?"

"Yes what is it. I am in kind of a rush. Let's walk and talk at the same time."

"Oh can you walk a bit slower for me. I can't keep up with you," I said jogging just to keep up with her. But I couldn't keep up, running out of breath, as she yelled back to me, "I'm in a rush. Sorry."

As she left me behind, I was left with a familiar feeling, used to being left behind. I could not keep up with others in studies or physical activities. I was struggling to achieve even the most basic tasks that many take for granted. How would I ever achieve anything in life? All

I kept asking God Almighty was one question, "Would I ever be able to keep up with everyone in life? Please God,"I don't want to be left behind. Don't leave me behind!"

> **Psalm 40:17 But as for me, I am poor and needy; may the LORD think of me. You are my help and my deliverer; you are my God, do not delay.**

ALL BECAUSE OF A DRUNK DRIVER! PLEASE DON'T DRINK AND DRIVE

The Long Haul

Victor Grewal, graduate.

It was a title I could finally claim as my own when graduation day dawned.

I was giddy with excitement that morning, figuring this would be one of the best days of my life. I was so thankful to my parents for all of their love and support that got me through college. I thought back to the studying, diligence, and hard work it took to earn the library technology certificate. Nothing held me back from achieving my educational goals, not the discouraging remarks from one professor, nor my short-term memory deficit, or anything else in life would hold me back. It was a day to celebrate and a day, that at times, I thought would never arrive.

After getting my congratulations from my family, I listened to "Celebrate" by Kool and the Gang thinking about the endless opportunities in my future.

While the graduation ceremony took over three hours there was one speech that really affected me.

A young lady named Tiffany had this to say to her fellow grads: "I am quite honored to be here after all those years of hard studying. This was not my two-year community college but my four-year community college. It took me a while but I did it!" It reminded me that I was not the only one who took four years to complete this education.

After the ceremony I went to my dad and gave him a big hug. "Thank you dad. This is something I will never forget. Thank you for helping me to complete my assignments and helping me do my homework. This certificate in library technology really should have your name on it."

"No my son, you have worked and studied so hard to achieve this dream. You deserve all of the very best that life can offer."

At that point, with my father's stomach started bothering him, he and my mom got ready to depart, telling me to have fun that night with my friends Paul and Woo.

"Don't worry", Woo told my dad, " I am driving."

"Good. You have a good friend who takes good care of you," my dad said before leaving.

That night, as I was out and about with my friends I was very happy. All of us went to my favorite restaurants, one with some of the best Mexican-style food in the city. They had a dance floor, DJ to play music, and a complete bar.

"OK Victor, before this night even begins, please give me your car keys. I don't want you to even have them in your possession. I am going to take care of you tonight," said my friend, Woo.

As the night wore on, I was feeling a bit tipsy from the alcohol, but sang to myself:

"Feeling so happy tonight...

Under the moonlight...

I am the king...

I have achieved everything...."

My friends were so kind to take care of me and I spent the night at Paul's house, just down the street from the restaurant.

"Now let's see what will await me?"

"Thank you for driving me last night Woo," I told him the next morning.

"You're welcome. Anytime, Just don't want you to drink and drive."

"Oh you know I would never since of what happened to me at the age of 5."

They got me to my car and I went home, a bona fide college graduate with a certificate in library technology.

Life After College

Finding a job—that was my next challenge.

I had done everything possible to prepare for this moment, working and studying, putting my entire focus on finding employment.

While still volunteering at the library, I continued my job search. My resume was up to date and I wasn't about to let anything or anyone discourage my quest.

Mrs. D., the senior librarian where I volunteered, was great help, getting the correct application for me and telling me where to send it.

She told me, "Victor, you can fill out the application at home and bring it back when it is complete."

"OK thank you. I will fill it out as soon as possible. Is it OK if I turn it in next week?"

"Sure it is. You can also mail in the application to the office where they will review your application and decide if they want to give you an interview."

"OK thank you very much Mrs. D. I greatly appreciate all of your help. I can't wait to start working as a library technician in this library."

I was so happy to have this application in my hand. I drove home right away and started to fill it out.

With my dad's help, I filled it, going deliberately slow to make sure there were no mistakes. I kept God in the front of my mind for this moment which took many years of hard work, volunteering and perseverance to achieve.

I also went to a couple university libraries and filled out applications there. Now I was playing the waiting game, eagerly anticipating when I could go in for an interview.

"God has the perfect job for you Victor. You look so nervous. Please just relax, because once you have a job then you will always be working. Every stage in life has its challenges. We must wait patiently my son," my dad kept reassuring me.

"I know dad I know but sometimes I just feel like giving up."

"We must never give up son. People like you and I, who are disadvantaged, must be brave and keep our heads held up high. There is a light at the end of every tunnel. When I went to apply for my first job after I graduated from the University of Chicago I filled out at least 100 job applications. I got a lot of rejections but thankfully was accepted by one company."

He then referred back to the night of the crash which seemed to occur more and more often.

"Dad please don't look back. Let's keep our eyes focused on a bright future and all the good that is to come," I said trying to comfort him with my words.

"You're right son. Sorry.... My mind just sometimes does not accept the fact that I may never be able to walk ever again."

"I don't know what to say except that you are an awesome dad. Despite of what has happened to you and all the challenges you face you have always been so caring to the family."

"Thank you my son. And you are an awesome son. You have done so well in your life and am happy that God is helping you.

"No, God is helping you and I both. He has a lot of people to take care of! I am glad he has not forgotten about us," I replied with a smile.

While not working, especially at night, I spent a lot of time with my dad. His advice was usually helpful, and I liked helping him, preparing his medication, getting him his water or going over what to watch on TV.

Sometimes, if he was in severe pain, I would massage his arms and hands. At times, he would fall asleep as I was relaxing his body.

One night, we, or should I say (since he had fallen asleep), watched "Some Like It Hot," I thought what the future has in store for me. Where would I start a career, what would I be doing 10 to 20 years from now?

Romans 8:28 And we know that God causes everything to work together for the good of those who love God and are called according to his purpose for them.

The day after I completed filling out my application, I returned it to Mrs. D. who in turn would get it to the main library headquarters.

She explained it usually takes three to four weeks to respond after an application has been submitted and then they would send me a notice to take the library technician exam.

"Have you been studying for it?" she asked me.

"No, but I will now," I replied.

The morning before the test, my dad told me:

"Say a prayer son before you take the exam. God will help you and if this is not the right test for you then, God will steer you in another direction that will bring you happiness. Keep God in the very front of your mind at all times."

I was still a nervous wreck and was so concerned about being late, I made the half-hour drive with plenty of time to spare.

The test consisted of three sections: basic math, English and library job related questions but three weeks later, the results weren't what I had hoped for.

"Don't be discouraged son," my parents told me. "Everything will happen in time.

I told them, "I think I should take the test to become a library page for the county. I will at least get paid for doing that work that I am already doing."

"OK son that may be good," my dad said.

The following day I filled out the paper work that I needed to take the library page test. It was a basic test of how to organize materials according to the library classification system. Some books were by Dewey decimal system, others were shelved by author. It was the most basic test that I was sure that I could pass it – at least that's what I thought.

Knocking On Every Door
But No One Answers

The disappointment of not becoming a library technician was still fresh when I got the call to take the test to be a library page, two weeks after submitting the application.

Even if I had to start from the bottom, at least this job would kick start my career.

"Hi Mr. Grewal how are you?" the exam proctor asked before I took the test.

"I am doing good. Just a bit nervous of how I will do on this exam," I replied.

"Oh you'll do fine. Just relax, take a deep breath, and everything will be all right."

The proctor gave me a cart of 20 books to put in order and I had five minutes to get the job done.

Using all of the information from my college years and volunteering, I slowly started to put the books in order. I can do this... I can do this... I thought to myself. Soon time was up, I had completed the exam and I had a good feeling about how well I did.

Two weeks later, the results were in and I scored a perfect 100 percent on the shelving test.

But passing the test didn't automatically get me hired. I was now on a list of other qualified applicants, eligible to work in the San Diego County library system, when a vacancy opened up, I would be called and would go in for an interview.

"Look I received 100% on my shelving exam to work in this library. Now I just have to wait for a job opening."

I explained all this to my dad who was amazed to hear how many steps it would take to get hired for a full or part-time job.

"Well hang in there son. You will just have to be patient and just wait to see what happens. In the meantime, you should continue to study for your library technician test.

"Yes dad, I know. I will continue to study to pass that exam."

"Good, my son. I am proud of you and all that you are achieving in life."

"Thank you dad," I said as I gave him a big hug.

A month or two passed and the call finally came to go in for an interview. I actually knew the people who would interview me. One of the women was from the library I had and was still volunteering at. I felt fortunate to be interviewed by someone who knew my work.

"This is an interview for the county library. We currently have a part-time position open with benefits. We will be asking you questions based on your knowledge and experience working in libraries. Have you ever worked in a library before?"

"No I have not worked in a library with pay but have volunteered. I currently am volunteering and have for four years. I have experience in shelving materials, emptying the book drops, checking the books in the library, processing the newspapers and putting them on the shelves. I am also a graduate with my library tech certificate from the local community college. I do have all the knowledge there is to know to work in a library."

"What would you do if your friend came in the library and started to talk to you?"

"I would tell him or her that I can not talk to you now as I am working and I will talk to you later. I can not talk to you during working hours.

"OK, what happens if there is a situation that you can not handle or something that you do not understand. What would you do?"

"I would ask my supervisor on what to do."

"What happens if your supervisor is not there?"

"I would then ask a fellow co-worker on how to handle the situation."

"Do you have your own transportation or would you need to rely on someone for transportation?"

"I drive my own car and have a valid drivers license. I also just live right up the road from the library so it would be no problem to get to work."

"OK, thank you for coming in for this interview. We will let you know what our decision is in a week or so."

Once the interview was over and I said my good-byes, I felt there was a good reason to feel optimistic. My parents eagerly waited for me to come home and relate how things went.

"Dad and mom, I think I got the job. I answered the interview questions and just feel as if I did a great job. I think the people who took my interview were satisfied and will hire me."

Waiting to hear whether I got the job was difficult. One week later, the letter arrived but before I opened it, my mom told me to take God's name and say a prayer. "In case it's a no," she added.

"What! I can not believe my eyes. After all of those years of volunteering and studying they did not hire me. I almost do not feel like volunteering in that library anymore," I said, shocked by the news.

"Oh my, son don't give up, be strong," my dad said as we hugged. "Continue to volunteer Victor. Maybe this time you did not get the job but it will look good on your resume that you are and have been volunteering in one place. Just keep your head held high!"

"OK dad, thank you for your advice. I will try to stay positive even though I do not understand why in the world they did not hire me."

I showed up to volunteer the next day and saw the person who they hired instead of me. In the back of my mind I wondered what he had that I didn't? He was a young boy, still a teenager. It was a puzzle that I could not solve.

I asked the person who took my interview why they decided not to hire me. Their reply: the other candidate had more work experience.

I thought, how was I supposed to get a library technician job if they could not even hire me as a library page, an entry-level library job? Nevertheless, I continued volunteering, pretending all was well, a fake smile plastered on my face, hiding the hurt I felt on the inside.

Begging

Now what?

While I continued to volunteer, I looked at applying at other libraries. One, in particular, caught my eye.

It was one of the newest in the city, two stories, an outside loft for reading and a beautiful section for children with a big, open yard.

Yet, I still harbored the fear that whenever I interviewed, those in charge of hiring, focused entirely on my disability, instead of giving me a chance to show I could do the job.

I set aside all of my fears and decided to get an application at this beautiful place.

"Hi my name is Victor S. Grewal and I am here to pick up an application to work here," I said to the library technician at the front desk.

"Certainly, what position are you interested in applying for?"

"I will take any position that is suitable with my educational and work background. I graduated with a library technician certificate."

"OK, here is an application Victor. You may have a seat at one of these tables and fill it out."

"Can I take it home with me and fill it out and bring it back later?"

"No, you must fill it out here."

I wanted my certificate and other documents to be included, so I planned on returning the next day with a completed application.

On the way home, I envisioned myself working there, and thought, "Wouldn't that be awesome if I can get a job in this library? I can see all of this turn into a reality!"

"So son, did you apply at that beautiful library that you are always talking about?" my dad asked when I arrived.

"No, I couldn't because I need to have all my documents with me as I have to apply for the job."

I told him I would go back the next day to finish it.

The next day, I filled it out and made sure I did not miss a thing. It took me about two hours to complete since I was nervous doing it by myself.

"OK, I finished filling out the job application," I said as I handed it in.

I was told it would be passed on to the person who would contact me for the interview.

Before departing, I thanked her and shook her hand.

Upon leaving, I was hopeful. I kept praying that God would open this door for me.

Philippians 4:19 And the same God who takes care of me will supply all of your needs from his glorious riches, which have been given to us in Christ Jesus.

"So, how did it go?" my dad asked.

"I think they were quite impressed and I think they will call me in for an interview, or at least that is my hope."

"Yes all we can do is wait patiently," my father answered.

Two weeks later I received a call from the city library that I applied at.

"Hi, my name is Jane. I am the head of the circulation department at The City Library where you applied for a job. Currently we do have a few openings for library page. Would you be interested in this position?"

"Yes most certainly I am interested," I replied with great enthusiasm.

"OK great. Can you come in for an interview next Wednesday at 10:00 a.m.?"

"Oh yes, and thank you so much for this opportunity," I said excitedly.

My heart was dancing with joy, and my mind kept dreaming about the endless opportunities there would be for me to grow and the many things that I could do in this beautiful library.

I wanted to look my best, so on the day of the interview, mom ironed my shirt and pants and even found time to put a nice polish on my shoes.

My parents, as had been the case for previous interviews, wished me the best and as I was leaving, "Good luck son, and as the saying goes, 'Break a leg.'"

Parked outside the library for my 1:30 appointment, I waited for a moment, then took a deep breath and prayed to God.

I was ready.

The interview would include Jane and three other woman.

We met in the library.

"You are a bit early but that's OK. Let's walk to the office where we will have the interview. I think the other people who are going to take your interview will be ready as well. Please have a seat in this room."

I was introduced to the other three woman who would question me, all circulation coordinators and then Jane explained what was expected of me if I was hired: being responsible for shelving the library materials, emptying the book drops, and making sure the books and materials are in order on the shelves.

I had done all of that as a volunteer, explaining that I had five years of experience.

The next question nearly threw me for a loop:

"If you have volunteered for so long why have they not hired you?" Shriva, one of the circulation coordinators, asked me.

"Because they have not had an opening. I just now passed the library page exam for them so my name is on a list that they will call me from when an opening comes about," I answered but this was a partial lie. The reality that played in my mind was this: they hired someone else for the job and I still couldn't understand why? The awful word "disability" haunted me since I thought that was reason why I wasn't hired.

"Do you think your disability will affect your performance in doing this job efficiently?" Stella another circulation coordinator asked.

"No, my disability will not affect my performance in this job. If I did think that I could not do this job efficiently then why would I have applied for it? I have done this kind of work at the county library for years," I said as I tried to keep my cool.

I was asked "Suppose your friends come in to talk to you while you are shelving the books or working on another task such as shelve reading. What would you do?"

"I would tell them that I need to work right now and do not have time to talk. I really need to concentrate on getting this job done so I will talk to you later."

"What are the hours that you can work? On the application you put 'Open'," Stella asked me.

"I am open to work all hours. I can work any day of the week."

"OK that is good," Shriva mumbled.

125

"Do you have your own transportation or would you rely on anyone else to bring you to work?"

"I do drive my own car and do have a valid drivers license."

"OK well those are all of the questions we have. Is there anything else you would like us to know or do you have any questions?"

"Yes well I would like to say that I am bilingual and can speak English and Spanish".

"Oh really. Can you say something to us in Spanish right now?

"What would you like me to say?"

"Say please put the books on the shelf?"

"Pon los libros en estante por favor."

"WOW! That is very good," Jane said.

"So how soon would you be able to start working?" Shriva asked.

"As soon as you call me. When would you be making your final decision about who gets the job?"

"In a week or two we should have a response. If you do not hear from us then you may feel free to contact us. OK thank you very much," they said as I gave each a firm handshake as the interview concluded.

Going home, I felt good about the interview except for the part where they asked me if my disability would effect the way I would be able to do the job. Well, at least I was able to say that I am able to speak English and Spanish so that should help. I had mixed emotions whether I said everything to show I was the right person for the job.

I gave my parents a quick recap of the interview and they thought the answers were good.

"We must have faith in God Almighty and just know that his plans are the best. Only he knows if you got that job or not. If you didn't, then keep your head held high and keep trying in other places," my dad said.

I wrote a very nice thank-you note, expressing my gratitude for the chance for an interview and how much I was looking forward to hearing their decision.

Now, it was time to play the game I detested, the waiting game.

After two weeks, I finally called to see if a decision had been made. I had a sick feeling in my stomach the response would be, "No, we did not decide to hire you and have hired someone else."

I reached Jane, who said they were still interviewing candidates. She said I could call back in a week and added, " We did receive your thank-you letter. That was very nice of you. Thank you Victor. We'll be in touch."

Another week passed by and I called again.

"Hello this is Victor S. Grewal. May I please speak to Jane?"

"Yes this is Jane speaking."

"Hi, have you come to a conclusion on who you will be hiring?"

"No not yet. Thank you for being so persistent and for calling in to find out."

"OK I will check in again after a week."

"OK that sounds good. We should reach a decision by then," Jane replied.

Week after week I kept calling Jane and Jane kept telling me to call back. I must have called them a couple dozen times before they reached me.

And the news was good.

When the phone rang, I answered and recognized Jane's voice, becoming nervous.

"Hi, we have come to a decision on whom we should hire and we have chosen you. Can you come in next week on Wednesday at 9 a.m. for a brief orientation to show you the ropes?"

"Oh yes and thank you so much! I am so happy! I will be there on time and I will be the best employee that you have ever had." I was so happy, my heart was dancing with joy and I kept repeating "thank you God" over and over again.

I called the county library where I volunteered at for so many years and told them the good news. I had gained all of the experience I needed with the county library and thanked them for all they did for me.

"Ms. D I got the job at the city library. I can't believe it. They actually hired me!"

"That's great Victor. I am so happy for you. See what a little hard work can do?" she replied.

"I wanted to thank you and everyone else who works here. Thank you for all of your help and for teaching me so much about the library. I will never forget any of you."

I later got to say my goodbyes in person. When I drove off, I felt strange, leaving a place for the final time where I had volunteered twice a week for the past five years of my life.

A New Beginning: Hello City Library

My first day of employment was awesome as I had landed my first paid position in my line of work which was the library. All the hard years of studying was finally paying off! I met a lot of really nice people who really seemed to care for me, were always supportive and there to answer any questions I had.

"Hello Victor, are you ready to work? We have got a lot of it for you to do," Jane said.

"Yes I am ready to work and will promise to be an excellent employee."

Jane introduced me to Jeff, another page, who was instructed to show me around.

Jeff was heavy set, who also had a disability but not the same as mine. His was more mental than physical and his way of dealing with me was a bit different compared to

Jane. I noticed others with disabilities working at the Library and it bothered me; I thought Jane and other staff members would categorize me as having the same disability as the other employees.

Jeff showed me where all of the mystery books, DVDs and VHS tapes were, along with fiction books. On the second floor were reference books, which couldn't be checked out as well as non-fiction.

As we went downstairs Jane continued the tour. "Victor how did you like the tour so far?"

"It was good. I enjoyed it. I think it will take me a while to remember where everything is, this library is new to me."

"Don't worry, you can take your time and as you continue to shelve the library materials the more adjusted you will be in knowing where everything is."

The break room was my favorite part of the tour! There were refrigerators, vending machines, microwaves, tables, chairs, recliners, a TV and an outside seating area. I sat on the recliner for my very first break and thought to myself, "Nothing could be better than this. I have a job in the library, and that is all I have ever wanted."

I ran into Trish, the head librarian, who remembered me when I came to this library to check out books.

"Wow! You are finally working here!" She said with great excitement.

"Yes. I have been hired as a library page and this is my first day."

"I think that's great that you are working here. How do you like it?"

"I like it. I am just now getting acquainted with the library and where everything is. It is kind of confusing but I will get the hang of it."

Back in the circulation department it felt great to meet people who were so nice. It made working so much more enjoyable.

As Jane was taking the time to show me how to do my job, I felt happy and I appreciated how thoroughly I was being taught to do it. I was paying very close attention to the many details involved in the job and there was so much to digest. She was very patient with me, at one point asking, "Am I going too fast for you, Victor?"

"No," I answered, "This is so wonderful. I am already loving this!"

After giving me a thorough explanation regarding shelf reading, she asked again if I had any questions.

"No, everything is good. I feel very confident I can do this job. It just seems a bit overwhelming as there is so much to learn and do," I told her as we were walking up to the reference area.

"Yes, but don't worry. You will get used to it and everything will be OK," she assured me.

With my duties fully explained, asked to volunteer, and empty the book drops and fill the cart. I had a good first day of employment.

"Feeling blessed and feeling good just like I should. Thank you God Almighty for all of the blessings," I sang, driving home.

"Son how was your first day of work at the library?" my parents asked me as I entered the house.

"It was so fun and I am so happy," I responded with great joy.

"We are so happy for you son and that you are finally hired by this library and the door to your dreams has been opened for you. God has opened the door for you Victor!"

"Yes I am so happy!"

"OK. So to celebrate let's watch a movie together tonight," my dad suggested.

"How about 'Some Like It Hot?'" I suggested.

"OK that's fine. Since you got the job, you can pick out that movie even though we have already seen it a million times already."

That evening, as we watched, we were filled with happiness and great joy. I got a huge box of popcorn and offered my dad some but he reluctantly declined.

Since developing pain in his stomach he couldn't eat foods he enjoyed, staying up as late as he wanted to, and many other things. He was living a very restricted life style and it wasn't enjoyable to him at all.

"Oh my son, that popcorn smells so good. I wish I could have some. I'm just scared that if I do have any then I will have spasms in my stomach that will hit my gut and that hurts a lot."

"I'm sorry son that I sometimes tell you things that are not very pleasant at times. Here it is such a nice night for you full of happiness for your job and here I am destroying the atmosphere."

"No you are not dad. Remember all of us are here to lean on one another for support. I lean on you and you can lean on me. Just as the song goes by Bill Withers. Here I'll sing you a verse from the song.

Sometimes in our lives We all have pain. We all have sorrow.

But if we are wise We know that there's always tomorrow.

Lean on me when you're not strong.

And I'll be your friend. I'll help you carry on .

For it won't be long till I'm going to need somebody to lean on."

"Oh my son that was a beautiful song."

"Well the lyrics are so true. Whenever I need help, you are there for me too. I always lean on you too."

"Thank you my son. Let's enjoy this movie."

As the movie played we enjoyed every laugh and enjoyed the night as we celebrated all that I had accomplished in life with the help of God Almighty.

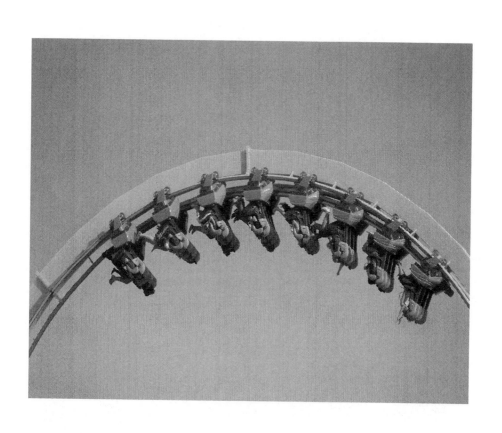

Working To Get Nowhere?

As I settled into my work routine, it began to dawn on me I would be much better off doing a less-physically demanding job.

The shelving took me longer than other people since I could only use my right hand and had limited use of my left side. I was also pushing carts, which put additional stress on my body.

My supervisor, Jane, saw that the shelving was taking longer than expected and asked I do it quicker.

As I continued to shelve, I tried to get faster, and faster while continuing to be accurate as possible. The 15-minute breaks I got were hardly enough time to rest.

"Oh mercy, God please help me get through this shift. My body may be weak but you make me strong."

After months, I felt I needed to apply for other jobs in the library that I felt qualified to do, including library technician. There was an opening for library clerk whose duties involved checking materials in and out of the library, renewing materials by phone, collecting fines and fees and responding to other general inquiries by patrons about account activity.

In my mind, I thought how relaxing it would be to just sit at a desk and check books in and out of the library, renew materials by phone, and then work would be like heaven. No more walking around, shelving materials, emptying book drops or anything physically straining. What I didn't know was that now the same place that I had planned to be at forever until the day I retire would be the same place that would turn into a living hell.

While I continued to work, all I could think about how these carts of books were chained to me and how much I yearned for a desk job that would be easy on my body.

As I would walk the halls, to my right were the library clerks, at their desks and to the left were the library technicians at their desks, all sitting comfortably, yet I was the one with a disability trying to carry on doing the best I could.

I couldn't figure out why I was being passed over and not given the promotion I deserved. I went to college and earned my library tech certificate to work at a desk. I never dreamed I would be stuck pushing around carts of books and other materials. I knew I was much smarter than this and I felt they were categorizing me with all those who had mental disabilities.

I had to face the painful realization that I was being discriminated against, something I never thought I would have to face.

I saw so many people, some as young as 19, get promoted to the position I had applied for. I couldn't understand why those with so little experience were being promoted before me. It was a mystery to me and something that lingered in my mind as I asked God in bitterness: "Why not pick me to do the job? Why are they doing this to me?"

I eventually confronted Jane, asking her why I had been passed by for a promotion to this job that I had applied for.

"Victor, what makes you think that you are qualified for this position as a library clerk?"

"I did this kind of work at the county library as a volunteer for many years. I have the experience in doing this kind of work and I also have a library technician certificate that I graduated with at a local community college. I am fully qualified."

"Sometimes life is not fair Victor and you may apply for this position once again if the job does become vacant again. I also have noticed how your shelving is not up to par as of yet. You need to shelve faster and be more accurate when you put the books on the carts to the shelves. From now on let me check your cart before you put them away and when you shelve, put the books face up so I can check them. In order to get a promotion from one department to the other your shelving must be 100 percent perfect."

When I pointed out other carts had errors, yet these people were promoted, she changed the subject.

"Well Victor, they had other qualifications that got them the job."

"Like what qualifications?"

"Sometimes life is not fair Victor. Can you please shelve those carts over there."

I felt singled out; none of the other pages were having their carts checked by Jane or other staff members. I felt lonely, isolated and not valued. I remembered back to the first day on the job and how I felt. I tried to rekindle the moments and keep my spirits up.

"Dad, what should I do?" I said one evening after work, "I have been working as a library page for eight months now but have not been promoted. Other people are being promoted who have not been there as long as I have."

"My son, I have a feeling that they are putting you down because of your handicap."

"No, no, I won't hear of it. I am not handicapped. I am just like everyone else. I just want to know why, why, oh God all I want to do is die," I said in desperation.

I was sick and tired of being disabled and viewed as having a handicap.

"Oh God please give me the courage to continue living this life," I said as I looked up towards heaven. "I know after this life, I will be in a better place, so please LORD take me now. I don't want to live anymore. I have suffered too much already. Oh God why me?"

After an hour my dad came to my bedroom door. "Oh son are you OK?" he asked me.

With tears running down my face, "No, does it look like I am OK? I am so sad right now dad and I have no control of this life and what people do to me."

"Everything is going to be OK," he said giving me a hug. People like you and I have to have more understanding of other people. Have courage my son and be brave."

He suggested we read the bible together, that it would bring peace to our minds.

Colossians 3:15 Let the peace of Christ rule in your hearts, since as members of one body you were called to peace. And be thankful.

"See son, here this passage is instructing us to always be thankful. God will bring you peace. All we need to do is trust him. Look at all he has given you. You have family, friends, and relatives who love you. All of us love you Victor. Now I suggest you go and work out at The YMCA. It will reduce your stress and make you feel good.

"OK dad, and thank you for helping me in my times of sadness."

"Why, of course my son. Remember we are a team."

Going to the Y has been a part of my life for years. Since 1987 it has become my home away from home.

When we first moved to California and got settled, the first thing my parents did was bring me there. I was first introduced to the pool as my parents encouraged me to learn to swim. They even got me a few swim lessons. Following instructions from my dad, I tried my best but it was difficult.

"Oh dad this is very hard to do," I said.

"Keep trying son. You will get the hang of it. Practice does make perfect."

In addition to swimming, I did other exercises in the weight room and took aerobic classes. I worked my way up to do three step aerobics classes in a row. I was determined to get and stay strong. I did not let anything hold me back. I lifted weights and did extensive 30-minute cardio sessions on the stair master. My family was amused by how much I could workout and encouraged me to keep it up, since it would help me to walk better. I loved the feeling of working out, reducing stress while allowing me to cope with the ups and downs of my life.

But not even this place was my safe haven. From time to time there would be someone who would put me down.

"Hello."

"Hi, how are you?" I responded to this stranger.

"Are you retarded?" he asked.

"No, I am not retarded. I was involved in a car crash by a drunk driver. That is why my left hand and leg are like this."

"You know," said my friend Brian, sitting nearby, that is not a very nice comment you made to my friend."

"Oh I am sorry," the man apologized.

I sat quietly and did not say anything. Brian continued to talk, "You know it's not his fault he is like that."

"Shhhh. Please Brian, it's OK. Please don't say anything else or I will start to cry. My heart is aching," I mumbled as he was trying to stand up for me.

"OK Victor, only trying to help you out."

"Thank you Brian."

Dad Tries To Help Solve The Mystery

My frustration, at the library reached such a point, I needed outside help.

So, it fell to my dad to try to straighten things out. He sought out the head of the library and was introduced to Jeffrey, assistant director of the library.

"Hi I am here to talk to you about my son Victor and want to understand the reason why he is constantly turned down for the jobs he is interviewed for?"

"Certainly let's go upstairs to my office. Here let's go up the elevator."

"He is highly qualified, has a library technology certificate from a local community college and has volunteered in the county library for many years," my dad said.

"OK, I will look into it. The next opening he should be able to get," Jeff said giving my dad false hope.

My tax attorney, Milu, even stepped in the library and tried to scare them.

"Hi my name is Milu and I am Victor S. Grewal's attorney. Here is my card," he said to the library clerk as he walked into the library one day.

After the visit from Milu, I was called into my boss's office. Jane was obviously shaken and telling me that the library had their reasons why I was not hired for other jobs.

My anger then spilled over. "I don't understand what those reasons are."

Jane abruptly changed the subject, asking if I was going to take the library to court.

"I just may have to. I am doing the library job very efficiently, and don't know why I would be passed by?"

"Well if you feel the need to go to court to resolve this issue then you can," she replied still looking a little fearful.

I always kept God in my mind during this trying time. Why was the library holding me back?

On Sundays I would go to church and ask pastor Roberts to pray for me, requesting the same prayer every time.

"Certainly Victor. Oh father and LORD Jesus only you know what is going on in Victor's heart. Please find favor in him and bring him peace of mind that you are going to take care of this situation and every situation that he may endure in life. Please put him in the job that he wants and if this is not the job for him then please lead him to a job that he will find satisfaction and enjoyment in. In your name we pray. Amen."

I often used to ask God "Why? Why me? I want to die because this life is so unfair and no one cares. Oh LORD, no one cares but you. I am all alone in this battle to stay alive and to survive.

Galatians 5:22-23 But the fruit of the spirit is love, joy, patience, kindness, goodness, faithfulness, gentleness, and self control. Against such things there is no law.

Galatians 5:22-23 became a way of life for me in the library and in all aspects of my life as nothing came easy for me. And, as far as achieving my dreams, some of them I had to walk away from. Thanks to a drunk driver, those dreams were shattered.

The next day, Milu wrote a letter to the library asking why I was turned down on every job I applied for. He also wrote that he would have to sue if nothing was done about the situation.

As I mailed the letter the following day, I felt very nervous and did not know if this was the right thing to do. I just kept repeating to myself, "God Almighty, only you know what will happen. Please help me to get the job I want with the help of this letter."

I went to work the next day, feeling a little nervous. I almost knew that things would not work out and I would be hassled by my boss. At this point, I felt this was a war I was waging, a war I hoped no one else would have to face. I felt everyone against me but God Almighty.

Psalm 3 O LORD, how many are my foes! How many rise up against me! Many are saying of me, "God will not deliver him." But you are a shield around me, O LORD: you bestow glory on me and lift up my head.

To the LORD I cry aloud, and he answers me from a holy hill.

I started my shift at 1 in the afternoon, emptying book drops, then shelving materials, shelf reading, organizing materials, etc. It was nerve wracking for me since I did not know when or what they were going to tell me when the letter arrived.

The next day I was still nervous about the situation when I got home that night.

"You look like a nervous wreck," my dad told me. "Let's watch TV tonight. You can pick out a movie that you would like to watch."

"Ok dad. Thank you but I don't think any show will take away the nervousness I feel inside my heart."

"Relax Victor. Please remember God is going to take care of everything. Let us put all of our trust in him. Look how far he has brought you in life. God is by your side my son."

As I lay down to sleep that night, I prayed, "Please God, let me get the job I want in the library and please allow all of this to go smoothly. I do not want to get terminated or hassled by anyone. I just want to be treated fairly, oh God Almighty. Please help me."

Then it occurred to me, what a big job God Almighty has. He has to take care of the entire universe. I wonder, what number I am on his priority list? In my mind I kept praying over and over again. Please keep my heart alive. Let me never give up my faith in you. As I kept wrestling with all kinds of thoughts and emotions, I fell asleep.

After a somewhat good nights sleep, I was again scheduled to work at 1. I really did not feel like going in because of how ugly the atmosphere had become.

To buoy my spirits, I called my friend, Paul, for some emotional support, minutes before my shift started.

"Hi Victor. I am good. I was getting ready to have lunch. What's going on? You sound so sad."

"Oh Paul, I really don't want to go to work today, but my dad tells me to go to work. I don't want to fight this battle any longer. I don't want to face these people any longer who despise me and only look down upon me."

"Be brave Victor. You will be fine. Don't forget they cannot fire you. Just keep doing your job. The best you can and good things will happen," he reassured me.

"OK thank you Paul. Just by talking to you I feel much better already."

As I hung up the phone I said these four words "Please God Help Me" and put a fake smile on my face.

"Victor before you start working I want to talk to you. Can you please follow me?" Shriva one of my supervisors asked me.

"Sure," I responded, a little nervous about what was going to happen.

I followed her to the second floor where I met Heather, the library administrator.

"Please have a seat Victor," Heather said.

"Victor this is a very sad day for us. An extremely sad day that we are going to have to let you go. We were hoping to have a long relationship with you but we feel you are not suitable to work with us. We received this letter from your attorney who wants to know why you are not been given a better job in this library. I, along with Jane have told you so many times of why you cannot have a better job in this library. We feel threatened by this letter," Shriva said.

"Well, I don't understand why I am not been given a better job. I have all of the qualifications," I responded.

"It's over. Please sign here and leave the library," Heather said.

As I signed the paper, it was like shattered glass that could not be put back together again, my dream of working in the library closed forever.

"Now, one more thing," Heather added, "You cannot come back to this library ever again to check out books or use the library in any way."

My heart sank immediately after she said this.

"I was not planning to come back to this library."

I actually felt relief, knowing I wouldn't have to deal with these people. I also called Paul to tell him what happened.

"What they can't... they couldn't have.

"But they did. What can I do? I think I will have to call my lawyer now for wrongful termination."

"Why don't you come over here. I'll take you out to lunch."

"OK but I don't think any amount of food is going to fix this situation or make me feel better," I said as I started to cry.

"Oh Victor it's OK. Don't worry about anything. Everything is going to be OK."

As I drove to his house I saw children getting out of an elementary school that was close to his house. "Oh LORD I pray that all of these kids future will be bright and prosperous. Let them excel and do well in life," I said, remembering my childhood.

Paul was sympathetic. "Hi Victor how are you? Or no wait you don't have to answer that question. All I want to say is that I am sorry for what has happened."

"So am I Paul. I want to go to the restaurant down the street so that I can get drunk and forget this day ever existed," I said sadly.

"But then you have to drive," he replied

"No all I want to do is get drunk, lay down, and die. This life is not meant for me. Everyone hates me."

"Oh Victor don't feel that way. We all love you. Where would I be without your friendship?"

"I still have to call my dad and let him know what happened."

"Hi Dad,"... I said sadly as he answered.

"Hi Son. What's wrong? You sound so sad," he responded with concern.

"Dad they fired me. The City Library fired me. See I told you they would. We should have gotten a lawyer right away."

"Don't worry we still will hire a lawyer for wrongful termination. They will have to answer for what they have done."

"But don't we have to forgive our enemies? That is what the bible teaches us."

"Yes but they have done great harm to you Victor. We don't want them to harm anyone else," my dad responded.

"Yes, but I don't ever want to have to face these people ever again or even look at them as we try to battle this out in court. To look at them is like poison to my eyes."

He asked me to come home and discuss things further, but I told him I was with Paul, getting some lunch.

Paul and I got a seat at the bar, a part of the same restaurant where we celebrated my graduation from college. It felt strange, to be where I once was so happy, just starting out my career but now sad, fired from a place where I thought I could build my career and now wondering what to do with my life.

"Hi Simi I would like to have a bottle of beer," I told the bartender.

"OK Victor you look sad and distraught and worried. Is everything OK?"

"No. I lost my job. The library I was working for fired me and I need to figure out what to do," I replied feeling sad. "I need a shot of whiskey too."

"Victor, now don't drink too much. Are you driving?"

"No he is not driving. We will call the cab. Victor you know you shouldn't drink so much alcohol."

"What else can I do? I need to forget about all my problems. I hate my life. No one loves me," I said throwing myself a pity party.

"Victor I love you," Simi said as she came on the other side of the bar to give me a hug. "God loves you too. We all love you. Don't ever feel so sad because we all love you."

After I was done having a bottle of beer and a shot of whisky, I started to calm down. Reality hit me hard as I wondered what my plan would be from here. As Paul rode with me in a cab to my house, he kept reminding me of how bigger and better plans would be in my future.

"Hi Mr. Grewal here is your son. He drank a little bit too much and I brought him home in a cab," Paul told my dad as he answered the door.

"OK thank you Paul," my dad replied as I clumsily walked in the house.

"Oh Victor I'm glad you have a such a good friend as Paul. He did not let you drive home," my dad said as he gave me a hug as I began to cry.

"Oh dad what ever happened. How awful. What am I to do with my life?"

"We have to depend on God Almighty Victor. He will show us the way. Remember his will, will be done on earth as in heaven."

"We have to hire a lawyer to help us sue this library that has done me so wrong", I said hastily." I am kind of glad I am gone from the library as now I do not have to put up with them anymore but feel sad as they killed one of my greatest dreams. "

"Don't you worry my son. We will sue them and make them pay for all the suffering they have caused you."

ALL BECAUSE OF A DRUNK DRIVER! PLEASE DON'T DRINK AND DRIVE

Life's Unexpected Ending

So, I had no job. I was uncertain and uneasy about my life and where I was headed. I prayed, asking God for guidance. "Oh please LORD, lead me where I can see the blue skies that will bring me prosperity. I don't ever want to go down a path where people don't like me and where I am put down like I was in the library."

As I did every morning, I went and saw my dad.

But his response this time scared me.

"Oh son, I am having extreme chest pain and am even having trouble breathing at times. Can you go with me to the doctor today to see what is wrong?"

"Sure I will dad. We need to call the lawyer as well."

"Please son, I am in dying pain now. Let's deal with this first and then we will call the lawyer."

"OK dad," I said feeling discouraged and scared as to what could be wrong with my dad this time. It reminded me of when he first had stomach problems in 1991 which was 13 years ago.

On the way to the hospital, I prayed that nothing very severe would come out of this.

We were led to a room where the doctor examined my father but it was cold, my dad started to shiver, asking for extra blankets on legs with no muscle tone.

The doctor asked my dad how he was doing.

"I wish I was feeling better. Doctor, my stomach is hurting a lot and at times I have trouble breathing. It actually hurts when I breath. A spasm erupts in my stomach."

OK let me run a few tests here to see what is happening. Your son can step outside and wait."

While hoping for good news, I wasn't completely surprised when the doctor came out after half-hour examination. My intuition told me something was awfully wrong. He told me my dad had developed stomach cancer. That was the bad news but he also told me the cancer was contained and had not spread to other parts of his body.

All worries about my future disappeared immediately. I was only concerned about my dad and how we were going to get through this.

When my dad was wheeled out, I gave him a hug.

"Oh dad I can't believe this!"

"Neither can I. Please don't tell your mom or brother. I will tell them," my dad instructed me.

"OK dad I won't. I promise."

"I will need everyone's help more than before. I feel so bad all this is happening."

"Oh dad don't feel bad all of us are here to help one another out. You have helped me out so much all these years. We are a team dad and we must stick together like glue."

On leaving the hospital and helping him get in the car my mind flashed back to how many times he had transferred himself to and from the seat in the car. All those years put a strain on his arm muscles as he told me from time to time over the last five years.

"Oh son, this life is so hard sometimes. All we can do is have faith in God Almighty and that he will pull us through difficult times. You and I know how hard life can be at times. Please my son, remember my words! Have trust and faith in God Almighty."

"Yes dad. You have told me that many times before."

"Well I am telling you one more time son because I care for you and no one else will tell you all of the things I tell you. I am scared. I hope I will not suffer very much throughout all of this. Just imagine, I once fought in the army before my marriage. I started out as a lieutenant, working up to the rank of a major. I did not even get a single scratch on my body but then this car crash happened, I became paralyzed, and now I have cancer of the stomach. What a life that I hope, and pray, no one else has to experience."

I had never seen my dad in so much anguish as tears rolled down from his cheeks. I tried to say words to uplift him and make him feel better.

"Don't worry dad, you are going to make it through this because if God brought you through so much in life then why wouldn't he bring you through this? I am always here to help you dad."

Once home, he reminded me to not say anything to the rest of the family. As we went into the house, my mom was outside in the backyard drinking tea and my brother was at work.

We slowly went to the backyard where my dad told my mom the awful news that no one ever wants to hear. Not surprisingly, she started to cry but tried to be optimistic.

"Oh Gary, everything will be OK. All we need to do is have faith in God Almighty. I am always here for you," my mom said mournfully.

He replied, "What else can we do but have faith in The LORD and put all of our trust in him. He will bring us through every battle in life."

Psalm 62:8 Trust in him at all times, you people, pour out your hearts to him, for God is our refuge.

My brother arrived from work, overheard this conversation and wondered what the crying and tears were all about.

"Oh son," my dad looked up to my brother, I have bad news!"

"Yes dad what is it. What's going on here? Can someone please let me know?" he said in panic, with no clue of what was going on.

"I have cancer of the stomach son. The doctor gave me one year to live."

"OK so now everyone knows. Please do not tell anyone else. Especially do not tell your grandma (in India with a bad back). Traveling all the way from India, with a bad back, would be very hard on her.

"OK dad, we promise," my brother and I said, looking at our father in disbelief as the reality of the news slowly sank in.

That evening, we sat in the master bedroom and prayed, asking God for help and comfort in this difficult time.

Psalm 25:1 In you, LORD my God, I put my trust.

Doctors... Doctors... Doctors

Our family had spent more than 20 years dealing with challenges, big and small. Now, cancer growing in my father's stomach, was the latest roadblock to overcome.

The following weeks were filled with many doctors appointments, going to the hospital to get ready for surgery, and tons of prayer that were in all of our hearts 24/7. I couldn't comprehend my father had developed this insidious disease. He had eaten right, drank alcohol in moderation, was very health conscious, and had exercised daily. He lead a healthy lifestyle despite the paralysis over the last 23 years. This was very perplexing for me to try to figure out.

The idea of seeing more doctors left him depressed.

"Looks like I will be seeing many doctors from now on. Oh son, I am so sick of seeing doctors. Looks like my life is ending in that way."

"Dad, you are going to make it through this and get rid of this cancer," I said reassuring him that everything is going to be all right.

"I sure do hope so."

"I know so dad. All we must do is pray and everything will be OK."

Once in the hospital, my fears took over. There were many cancer patients and my mind imagined what was going on in the room where my father was examined.

"So now what dad? What is the next step?"

"Now comes the day of the surgery (Tuesday) in a few days. Oh son, I am scared."

I had never heard my dad say those words from my dad. In my heart, I always said: "Please LORD bring him through this illness and let him be rid of this." But realistically, I knew this would be his final battle as he had been through so much since the crash. I had a gut feeling his body would not be able to fight off this cancer.

Since the 1982 crash, my dad had faced many obstacles, and his upcoming surgery would be the next.

The surgery, in order to eliminate most, if not all the cancer, would require a large portion of his stomach to be removed.

When he awoke from the anesthesia, the family was there for him.

With a feeding tube that went down his throat, it was difficult for him to speak, yet he asked my brother about his job, asked my mom about the house and told us he wanted to go home. My brother told him, "Don't worry about me. Our main concern right now should be to get you home."

"All of us miss you dad," I added.

When visiting hours were over, I glanced back as we were leaving and said to myself, "Dad you're going to make it home."

Soon, he was released from the hospital but before coming home, was placed in a nursing home for two days. He still had to get nourishment through his feeding tube. He hated being at the nursing home and hated having to depend on the feeding tube.

My mom made arrangements to hire a caregiver who knew about the feeding tubes and how to deal with them.

When he finally came home, he was miserable, dealing with feeding tubes, his stomach still in knots, and in severe pain. The saving grace: he knew my brother, mom, and I were there for him.

His caregiver, Melissa, helped him in the bathroom, changed the dressing from the surgery, and also made sure the feeding tubes were in place. He hated the idea of having a caregiver but my mom thought that it would be good until he became adjusted in the house.

"Jessie, I appreciate the caregiver so much but really do not want to have one. I can take care of everything myself," he complained one night.

"Gary, she will help us for a few weeks. My back hurts a lot too and I just want to have her around to assist you. Until all of us get adjusted to these feeding tubes and everything else we will need her assistance."

"I don't like these feeding tubes. I am going to ask the doctor if he can remove them. They are very inconvenient and they are always getting in the way of everything."

"Gary, please don't get them removed. It will only do harm to you and your diet."

That night, after everyone went to bed and the house was silent, I said a prayer before I got into bed:

"Down on bended knees I pray that The Good Almighty LORD help my dad through this time of healing and that he remain calm and feel no pain as he had experienced enough pain in his life. Please LORD I know that you all call us home one at a time and we all have our time to die but I just want to say Thank you LORD for giving me such a loving father who out all the pain that he experienced in his life has always managed to smile. Please help him to beat this cancer. I hope the doctors were able to remove the cancer and that he may return to his normal way of living. He has been my source of strength when I was weak, has cheered me on in every victory that I made, and has been there for me through every obstacle that I faced. If it is ever his time to go, I want you to know this LORD. I am thankful for my dad and I am thankful we've been a team, always helping one another out. Thank you God Almighty for such a loving father!

Amen!"

* * * *

My dad's life after surgery was full of changes.

I remembered the years when he was able to use the bathroom independently and be ready by 8 or 9 in the morning. Now, with his stomach problems, bathroom procedures took him a few hours to complete.

His diet was even more restricted then before the cancer diagnosis. He took a medication that was in powder form that he would mix with a glass of water. The taste was awful, very bitter and he hated it. He would make the most disgusted face while taking it down his throat.

"Oh dad that looks so painful to take that medicine," I observed.

"Yeah it does not taste good at all. But if it does get rid of the cancer and gives me more time to live well then, it is worth it."

"That is all of our hope dad. All we can do is hope," I replied.

I also noticed a change in his personality. He was not as outgoing and was slowly losing that optimistic trait that he had carried with him for all those years.

One day, I asked how he was doing. His reply saddened me.

"Oh son I'm not feeling so good today. I feel very weak. I don't even feel like doing anything. I don't want to go for a drive or outside anywhere," he replied.

"Dad we must never give up. Remember that one time you told me that in your lifetime there would be a cure for paralysis and brain injury. Well dad I still have to see you walk someday. That has been my lifelong dream that I have not given up on. You are going to make it. All of us are going to make it through this nightmare! Please dad don't give up, promise me."

"Oh son, easier said than done. If you could only be in my shoes you would know how I feel. Let's just close our eyes and say a silent prayer. Say a prayer from your heart son. God is listening."

As we sat there, our silent prayers filled the room. After a minute he prayed out loud: "Dear Heavenly Father I know my days may be short here on earth but as for my son he has a whole life to live. Please God Almighty, direct all his paths to glorify your name. Show him the path to live to reach your kingdom in heaven. Help him in this life and to serve you. His disability, cure him of his limp and make his left hand strong. Please LORD take away his brain injury. His short-term memory deficit is so hard for him to deal with. We both know your timing is best and that is what we wait for. In your name. Amen!"

As the day went by and the discomfort of the feeding tubes continued to agitate him, he kept telling me of how he was going to get them removed. Then, he could eat regular meals.

My mom strongly objected.

"Please Gary, do not get the feeding tubes removed. You will need them," she begged him.

But he had his mind made up. I gave it one last try.

"Are you sure you want to do this dad? You really should think about this. What happens if you need them later on?" I said hesitantly.

"Son, I can do whatever I want to do. This is my life. I am so uncomfortable now. Please don't argue with me. Just help me."

As we drove down to the hospital, silence filled the car. Once there, he apologized for his foul mood.

"I can't wait to be rid of all of these things. I am sorry I have been a bit grouchy and not that pleasant. All of this is so hard for me to deal with."

"It's OK dad I get angry and upset too. My disability is very frustrating at times. I understand. No need to apologize. Remember we are a team," I said, giving him a hug.

He came out of the doctor's office after five minutes.

"Dad how do you feel?"

"I feel great son. Trust me, having those feeding tubes removed gives me so much more freedom. Let's go home."

Our return home, with the feeding tubes removed, did not make my mother happy.

"Gary what have you done. I told you not to remove the feeding tubes."

"Yes but they were not comfortable and they were just getting in the way."

"Don't say that I did not warn you to not take them out."

"OK OK...," my dad said as he pushed himself to the sunroom to do some exercises.

My dad was happier, that's for sure. No more hassles of having to worry about the feeding tubes getting in the way, no more long days and nights in the hospital, just at home now relaxing and hoping the doctors had taken out all of the cancer in his stomach.

Now that he was feeling better, my dad wanted to attack the cancer head on. That meant either chemotherapy or radiation. Either course of treatment worried me.

"Dad, you must not get either of them. It will kill you. You have already been through a lot in your life. Your body will not be able to stand all that treatment! Please dad if the doctor says you need it then don't because it will kill you. I don't want to lose you!"

"No, don't worry, Chemotherapy just makes you feel weak for a while but then the body will rebuild all of those cells and life will go back to normal."

> **1 Peter So then, since Christ suffered physical pain, you must arm yourselves with the same attitude he had, and be ready to suffer too. For if you have suffered physically for Christ, you have finished with sin.**

Three weeks later I went with my father to his doctor's appointment. We said a prayer before leaving the house.

"Oh LORD loving God Almighty please help my dad and I to relax during this doctors appointment. Knowing that you are in control of every situation in our life gives us great comfort. Please help my dad to get rid of this cancer that has caused him so much misery.

Please let this be pleasant. Amen."

As we drove to the hospital, my heart was racing, uncertain about what was to happen. As we arrived at our destination and I got his wheelchair out of the trunk I kept asking God to help my dad get through this.

While he went in, I waited and prayed: "Your will shall be done on earth as in heaven."

Shortly, he came out, telling me everything is going to be OK.

"No more cancer? It's gone,"I said, feeling excitement at this seemingly good news.

"I only said that everything is going to be OK. I did not say anything of the cancer yet. I will tell you more about it in the car."

That left me hanging in suspense while returning to the car.

"OK son, here is the situation we have at hand. I do have a little bit of cancer inside of me the doctors were not able to remove. It will require chemotherapy and radiation to get rid of the cancer."

"Oh no, now what?" I responded with great fear.

"Now I have to go and get chemo therapy and radiation done. As simple as that son.

Don't worry my son God is with our family. God is helping all of us."

"No dad you can't. I don't want you to. You can't. Dad I don't want to lose you!"

"OK son but it will only be good for me. Everything will be fine. The cells that die will rebuild and then I will be strong again."

"No dad, please you are not listening to me," I said with tears, "you are not strong enough to handle the chemo and radiation therapy. You have been paralyzed for many years. Your body is too weak."

To my surprise, he concurred.

"OK son. I won't get it. You are right," he said and gave me a hug.

Wedding Invitation At The Wrong Time

Taking care of my father was the No. 1 priority in my life and my family. Everything else had to be postponed.

The library situation on hold; finding a new job; going to The "Y' to exercise; everything was on hold until my dad recovered.

Everything was on hold until we received an invitation in the mail for my cousin's wedding in England.

There was no way we could go.

I told my mom I wasn't in the mood to celebrate.

"Neither am I," she responded sadly.

I kept thinking how God is in control of all situations and how He will take care of my dad while I am gone to England. It was a good opportunity, but an awkward time, to plan a trip anywhere. I prayed God would keep my dad safe until I could return. I had deep faith He would take good care of my father in my absence.

Hebrews 11:1 Faith is the confidence that we hope for will actually happen; it gives us assurance about things we can not see.

The next day I nervously asked my dad if he would mind me leaving to attend this wedding.

"No son, you go ahead. I will be OK. I feel fine. Don't worry about me," he said in his typical unselfish manner.

"OK, but I will be praying for you, dad. I am still nervous," I replied.

"Don't be nervous. Just remember, God, our heavenly Father is in control of everything.

I will be OK."

"OK, but promise me that you will not get any chemo or radiation therapy while I am gone.

That is the only thing that worries me."

"Don't worry my son I will not get anything done until you get back. If I do, then don't forget that God will take care of me."

"Dad remember your promise. Chemotherapy will kill you. I need you dad. I don't want to lose you," I replied giving him a hug.

In the following weeks, I kept praying and asking God if I should attend the wedding or stay home. Both my mom and I were torn by indecision, but ultimately we decided to take a chance and go. It wasn't easy but I knew God was going to take care of my dad for a couple of weeks so we could attend this joyful and happy event.

Still, it was difficult knowing I would be away for so long. At least my older brother would stay with dad for most of the time, flying over just three days, since he couldn't take extra time off from work.

On the day we left for England, I watched as my dad struggled to go to the bathroom. His atrophied legs hung limply to the side of the bed as he prepared to transfer to the wheelchair. It was hard to watch, seeing how difficult it was for him.

After saying our goodbyes, my brother drove us to the airport. I still felt uneasy, leaving my dad for such a long time. I reminded him to call if anything happened.

"Don't worry," he said as he dropped us off at the airport. "Have a nice trip."

Despite those reassurances from my brother, I couldn't shake the feeling that on my return, things would not be the same. I prayed constantly that God would take care of, and keep him safe.

It was exciting to be back in England for the first time since my childhood. It was cold and foggy with not much sunshine. I knew I would have to put on a happy face, when in reality, my thoughts and prayers were back in California, wondering how my dad was doing.

I eagerly greeted the prospective bride, my cousin Meena. "Looking forward to being a wife now and entering into the married world?"

"Oh yes I am quite excited. I will be happy forever."

"Good for you. I am so happy to be here on this very blessed occasion," I responded.

After a nice , long chat, we went to the kitchen where my mom and her sister were talking about old times and telling jokes to one another. It was difficult to keep silent about my dad's condition but my mom and I didn't want to ruin the happy atmosphere.

We always traveled alone as traveling for my dad was a huge inconvenience. He had to bring his shower and toilet chair, all of his medical supplies, and would need help to get in and out of bed because there would not be a motorized bed. He did not want to burden anyone and just wanted to be comfortable at home. Our relatives often questioned me as to why my dad did not come and that would always be my response.

We called my dad the first night of celebrations and asked him how he was doing.

"I am doing OK. I have decided to get the chemotherapy. Sorry, it is my decision and my sister has recommended a very good doctor. By the time you get back, my chemotherapy sessions will be over and the cancer in my body will be gone."

"Oh dad," I said in despair, "you promised me you would not get the chemotherapy. OK dad... it is your life. Just always know I love you."

My mom begged him to skip the treatment but without success.

"Don't worry dear, everything will be OK," he responded.

"OK Gary, but if things don't go well..."

"All we can do is leave it in the hands of God Almighty. Don't worry, enjoy your trip. Ricky will be there soon. Please don't worry about me," he said.

My brother arrived soon and told us everything was OK.

"So far so good. He had a few rounds of chemotherapy and seems to be a little bit weak. He is OK though he is still getting in and out of bed a little and exercising a little bit. His sister is with him now she is taking him to his doctors appointments for chemo," he explained to us.

"Oh good. Well I just pray that he be strong. Hopefully he will still be there when I get home."

"Oh Victor don't worry so much. He is fine. Just a little weak," my brother reassured me.

As for the wedding, we all had a good time. Then it was time to go home.

My brother, who left right after the wedding, was there to pick us up.

"How is dad doing Ricky?" I asked my brother.

"Well, he was doing really good until a few days ago. You'll see when we get home," he said as we headed back home.

Gravely Ill

I returned from England to see a father who would never smile again.

When we arrived home from the airport, the house was hot, the heat turned way up. We found my dad in considerable pain as the chemotherapy had caused blisters in his throat, hands, and feet.

"Hi dad, how are you doing?" I said as I approached his bedside.

All he could do was point to his throat and wave his finger to tell me that he could not talk. It saddened me to see all that he was going through. We all prayed that God help him to recover and to return to the person he used to be before cancer had robbed him of his health.

Revelation 21:4 He will wipe away every tear from their eyes. There will be no more death or sadness. There will be no more crying or pain. Things are no longer the way they used to be.

That evening I prayed the LORD heal him and make living comfortable for him. How much longer could he battle this disease that took away his smile and zest in life? Only God knew. All I could do, along with my family, was to pray.

As the weeks progressed, I saw my father decline; he was unable to eat, drink, or speak because of the pain of the blisters.

"Dad, don't worry this is just temporary. You are going to make it through," I said to give him hope that everything would be alright.

"I want to die. I don't want to live anymore," he whispered to me.

When those four words were uttered, I knew that his time to go to his eternal father would be coming soon. I prayed that God allow my dad to leave this earth without too much more pain. He had endured so much, already.

After weeks of not eating or drinking, we took him to the hospital, thinking they would replenish his body with fluids and he would come back home in a week or two.

"Don't worry Gary," my mom told him, "We will be praying for you and will be ready for you to come home as soon as you are stronger."

"Dad all of us love you and will be praying that you come home soon," my brother added.

I pushed him to get into his car and he never looked back at the place he lived for the past 18 years. All the memories, all of the material possessions left behind. The only thing he took with him was his love for God Almighty!

While waiting for him to get admitted, all I could do was remember what a great father he was to me. He had showed me strength and courage by the way he lived life after the crash

And, I was ever so thankful for the No. 1 lesson he taught me. "Depend on God Almighty. He will always be there for you."

Psalm 62:5 For God alone my soul waits in silence, for my hope is from him.

When he finally got a bed in the emergency room he was feeling very weak. We saw our neighbor Ronda, an RN, and she offered comforting words.

"Hi Gary," she said in greeting.

"He cannot speak very well as he has blisters on his throat," I explained to her.

"Oh dear, I do hope he gets well soon," she said sadly.

We met with the doctor who checked my dad's vitals and told us not to worry because everything looked good.

I was optimistic he would be home in a day or two. After getting settled on the second floor, we said goodnight and left. I felt really bad leaving him alone but I knew that God Almighty would take care of him.

The next day we discovered he had been moved to ICU south for less critically ill patients.

"Oh dad how are you doing," I asked going to his side.

"Oh Gary what happened?" my mom said, starting to cry.

"Oh dad, we hope that you will get better soon," my brother said as he patted my dad's shoulder.

As we sat there, all we heard was the beeping of the heart monitor and I kept an eye out to see if his heart was steady. We spent the whole day in the hospital, praying and reminiscing over better times.

"I will always try to follow the advice that you gave to me dad. How you always told me health is wealth and to eat your fruits and vegetables," I said.

Unable to speak he nodded and did manage to whisper: "It will be good for you my son".

"I will live my life in honor of you, dad. I will find a job where I can help and inspire people," I said lovingly, starting to cry.

"Thank you for all the love and support you gave to me dad," added my brother as he bent down to hug our dad.

"Dad, let me say the prayer that all of us said before we had dinner." As we folded our hands in prayer I began:

"Our Father, who art in heaven. Hallowed be Thy Name. Thy kingdom come, thy will be done, on earth as it is in heaven. Give us this day our daily bread and forgive us our trespasses as we forgive those who have trespassed against us; and lead us not into temptation but deliver us from evil. Amen."

That night, his vital signs started to deteriorate and was transported to the north ICU for more critically ill patients.

"Doctor what is happening. Why is his health failing so rapidly?" I asked.

"I don't know sir. We are going to sedate him. All three of you should say goodbye to your dad before leaving tonight because this may be the last time."

We went to my dad's side of the bed where he tried to talk but couldn't. He finally was able to whisper:

"I love you my sons. Please just know how much I love you. Lead a good life and..."

"Dad what is this? You are going to make it through. We will see you in a few days when you wake up," I said.

"No but this is just incase I don't wake up, I want both of you boys to know that I love you."

"We love you too, dad," my brother and I said at the same time.

"Thank you Jessie, for everything. Thank you for all the help you have given to me. I love you Jessie," my dad whispered to my mom.

"I love you too, Gary," my mom said. "I'll see you in a few days." She then gave him a hug.

As we left, I looked back at a man who had suffered so much, all because of a drunk driver, This man raised his family through the most difficult circumstances and I'll never forget those three final words that he said to me even though he was barely able to speak. "I

love you."

For the next four days, we visited him but he was motionless. My brother had to work but stopped by in the evening. My mom and I stayed by his side until visiting hours were over.

I noticed a radio that was left in the room. I thought about putting on some music that my dad used to sway his arms to so I went home and grabbed a Dean Martin CD he listened to many times. I played the song "That's Amore" as well as all of the other songs that were on the album. I kept hoping that he would wake up from his sedated state and start to sway his arms to the music.

On the fourth day, his heart rate dropped and he passed away. I held his hand and said, "Thank you dad. You are the man and I am your number one fan."

This is Mr. A who I grew very fond of and helped till his passing six years after I began volunteering. Some of his characteristics reminded me so much of my dad and he will always be that bright shining sun or star in the sky.

We built a very good friendship that I will always remember for the rest of my life.

I Work In Honor Of You Dad

Five months after my dad passed away, I started volunteering at A San Diego nursing home. I felt empty, with no direction. When my father was alive, I could funnel most of my energies into helping him. But he had gone to his eternal home and I was still here, trying to find meaning in my life.

A friend had gotten me an interview with one of her friends who worked at the nursing home. I was a bit apprehensive going in. Hopefully, this would be a new beginning for me.

I introduced myself, explaining I was there to volunteer.

While waiting, I saw many in wheel chairs, walkers, and some who looked capable of taking care of themselves, with a bit of assistance.

"Hi," said a tall woman with short brown hair who introduced herself as Nedra. "I heard through an employee who's name is Tammy that you would like to volunteer here with us."

"Yes I would. I would like to volunteer in honor of my dad who passed away of stomach cancer a while ago," I said.

"Oh did your dad live here at this place?"

"No my dad was left paralyzed from a car crash in 1982. I used to help him do many tasks such as make tea, make his bed, go on outings, pick up his medications and much more. Now I feel empty inside, not having anyone to help the way I used to for my dad."

"That is quite a story. I am the activity director. Would you be happy doing this kind of volunteer work and assist the residents in doing activities?"

I told her I would and went on to explain my own disability. I wanted to be as candid as possible about my handicap so there would be no misunderstandings down the road. When she indicated that wouldn't be a problem, it eased my mind considerably.

"You look very capable to me," she said as she walked with me to the theatre where the residents were doing an activity called balloon toss, then asked me to help with that activity.

164

"OK I can do that," I replied with excitement.

I met another woman, Tammy, who was friend's with Natalie, the woman who told me about The Nursing Home. Natalie was the one who referred me to come and volunteer.

"Natalie told me how eager you were to come and volunteer. We are glad to have you."

"Thank you so much, Tammy," I replied feeling grateful for God Almighty to bringing me to such a wonderful place.

"Wow this is kind of fun, I love this," I thought to myself. "Wouldn't that be awesome to get a job that I could get paid for. I can't believe people get paid for doing this kind of work with the residents. I will put in 100 percent effort into getting this job."

After helping with balloon toss, I assisted the residents in doing exercises upstairs.

I got great satisfaction knowing that I was helping and putting smiles on their faces.

Once I helped residents to the dining room for lunch, my day was done. I was going to give myself a limit of four hours a day for volunteer work since I did not want to get overworked or burned out. At the same time, it was gratifying that I was helping so many people, fulfilling my vow to honor my dad. I also wanted to show those in charge they won't regret putting me on their payroll. Still, I tried to maintain an even keel and not go overboard with hopes of getting hired.

I reminded myself to stay cool and when the right opportunity arises, I'll get the job. Remember, everything happens when God wants, not according to when I want it.

Galations 6:9 NIV Let us not become weary in doing good, for at the proper time we will reap a harvest if we do not give up.

That afternoon, when I got home, I couldn't hide my enthusiasm.

"Mom, I loved my time at the nursing home today. It was fun! I helped the residents to do exercises, lunch time, and a balloon toss activity. It was the best. I sure do hope that this does turn into a paying job some day."

"Don't worry son it will. Just be patient and God will open the door to that dream job. Do the best job that you can do and treat this volunteer work as if they are paying you."

"Oh I will mom. I am so happy now. I already love this kind of work."

I was puzzled over one aspect of this volunteer gig: Why did God lead me here instead of numerous others in San Diego County?

There was one particular resident I was drawn to, Mr. A.

I would stop by his room and he seemed not particularly happy.

One day, I asked him if there was anything I could do for him and he requested help in pushing his wheelchair to go outside. As I pushed, it felt like I was pushing my dad.

He guided me to an area where horses could roam which I thought was neat. There was a bench where we sat so Mr. A could get some heat from the sun.

We got to know one another.

"What is your name?" Mr. A asked me.

"My name is Victor."

"If you need to do anything else please go ahead."

"No. I want to be here only for you and that's it."

"Oh that's so kind of you. Thank you very much," he replied smiling. "Where shall we go next?"

"Lunch is around noon. Why don't we go inside and go to the dining room upstairs."

"OK that sounds good to me."

As we strolled through the hallways I saw the many residents but committed to give Mr. A

most of my love and attention because he so reminded me of my dad in the way he would talk, to the way he was so organized, and most importantly to how he always thanked me at the end of every day. I just felt as if I were with my own father when I assisted Mr. A.

When we arrived upstairs in the main dining room I sat him down and excused myself to pour drinks for everyone. Afterwards I went back to see if Mr. A was doing OK.

"I am doing good," he said.

"I am leaving soon. I will see you on Thursday though."

"OK, that's fine. Thank you for everything. I really enjoyed going outside and getting some fresh air."

"All my pleasure. I am so glad that you feel happy. When you are happy. I am happy too. I will see you on Thursday."

As I walked away, it gladdened my heart to have made someone's day because when I was with him, it felt as if I was with my dad and that was a terrific feeling to have. I figured I'll be hired someday, but for now this is my job, to take care of this resident until he passes away or moves out of the facility.

Just as the bible says, that is the way I will live. I keep it in my mind at all times.

Matthew 7:12 So in everything, do to others whatever you would like them to do to you, for this sums up the law and the prophets.

It would take a lot of sacrifice, and I would have to give up a lot of my needs, wants, and desires but I felt the need to want to do this to make someone else's day a little bit brighter. I was determined and committed and would take care of him despite of any circumstances that life may bring.

The Book Store

There was a great personal satisfaction in volunteering at the nursing home but the fact remained—I needed a real job in order to pay my bills.

I applied at several places: a book store, grocery store, and the music store and waited in anticipation to see who would call me for an interview.

When I got a call from the book store for an interview, it seemed like a perfect fit. Working there suited me so well, given my love for reading.

"OK, so by looking at your job application, it says that you volunteered at a library. Can you please explain to me what did you did over there?"

"I started to volunteer at the library, as I was studying to become a library technician. I used to empty the book drops, check the materials in and out of the library for patrons,

shelve materials according to call number, and assist patrons using the computer database to locate materials."

"Why did they not offer you a job if you volunteered there for so long?"

This was tricky. I did not want to get into a drawn-out explanation of my difficulties there.

"Because they did not have any job openings," I explained. "Also my dad got stomach cancer and I needed to take care of him. He passed away June 25, 2005."

"I am sorry for your loss and I do understand. We do have openings now for AM shifts that start at 6:00 AM for the shelving of materials. You also may assist customers in finding materials that they are looking for. Would you be interested?"

"Oh yes for sure."

"OK, then let me just call your references and I will get back to you."

I waited patiently for a reply and two weeks later, to my surprise, I got a call from the bookstore asking me to work for them.

"Can you be here tomorrow morning at 6?" Warren asked.

"Yes I can and thank you for this opportunity," I responded feeling grateful.

"You're welcome. We look forward to working with you."

I had a job.

But I would have to make some adjustments in my life. I knew I wasn't a morning person, yet that was obviously going to change. To get to work, then go on and volunteer at a nursing home and take care of Mr. A, would require me to be up by 4:30. It would be difficult but not impossible.

Luke 1:37 "For nothing will be impossible without God."

That night before my first day of work, I said a prayer to thank God Almighty for his love and guidance: "Thank you LORD for this new employment opportunity. I hope I will be able to do everything and still have energy left at the end of the day. Working and volunteering may not be easy but at least I have you God Almighty to help me through this time and through all the times in my life. Amen."

That morning, I arrived to find a number of employees waiting. Among them was a woman, Lilliann, who introduced herself and asked me how I was doing.

"I am good just a bit tired and sleepy. It's nice to meet you. My name is Victor S. Grewal. This is my first day on the job."

"Nice to meet you as well. Welcome aboard."

I then met the manager, Madge, who showed me around.

After we finished setting up my password we went to the back to the stocking room where all of the materials were kept to be put out in the store for the customers to purchase. There were huge carts of inventory. It was pretty intimidating .

Madge explained their shelving protocol and concluded: "Any questions please don't hesitate to ask."

Everything on that first day sounded pretty good to me. I felt excited to returning to the workforce after so much time of being unemployed finally I had found my niche and thanked God for guiding me to such a wonderful place.

Psalm 106: 01-Praise the LORD, for he is good; for his love endures forever.

It was hard doing both a paying job and a volunteer job but I knew what really fueled my passion. My future would be in the nursing home as I knew I wanted a job where I could help and inspire everyone. I also wanted to continue to help Mr. A for as long as he was there.

I loved the staff at the book store and they were so nice to me. I shared what had happened to me and they encouraged me to write this book, now to share with others.

After years of just helping Mr. A, I also wanted to focus on volunteering and doing activities work, something I was sure I could enjoy doing. I asked the activities director, Darlene, if I could help her out in doing any activities as well as my duties with Mr. A.

She agreed to let me help out, doing table games, tea parties, ball toss, and other engaging activities that the residents liked to do.

This was my mission: get a paying job at the nursing home. Deep down I knew it was not going to be easy. It would be filled with many ups and downs like a roller-coaster ride.

One cannot snap his fingers and have the dream come true. It takes work, hard work. And, that was the realization for me, as I worked in the bookstore in the morning, then went to the nursing home as a volunteer. That 4:30 a.m. wakeup call was tough.

I prayed everyday that all of the work I was putting into the nursing home would translate into a paid position. I remember my dad telling me how he used to juggle his busy schedule of working, going to school in the evenings and still have time for us . It was the same for me, working towards my dream.

The second day, I again struck up a conversation with Lillian who inquired as to how I was doing. I gave her a rundown of my busy schedule, working at the bookstore, then volunteering at the nursing home. She was impressed.

"You are a very busy person," she responded.

One of Lillian's duties was to take care of the newspapers in the morning, a task that I wanted to handle. She said she would show me how.

"Great. I love to learn how to do new things. I would love to learn how to do this," I responded.

Just then, someone new walked in, another manager names Bella, and I introduced myself. "Nice to meet you. I look forward to working with you," she said.

While I was shelving books, Bella walked past me as I was shelving the books and made sure I was doing my task the best I could.

"Are you doing OK Victor?"

"Yes. Just trying to keep up with the pace," I responded while still working .

"Don't worry Victor. You are doing great. Just do the best that you can. That is all that I ask,"Bela said to me with a big smile. "You bring a lot to this bookstore, you really do."

At 8:45, after our break, we gathered for a morning sales meeting we'd discuss the sales for the previous day's take, sales goal for the day and sales techniques that would increase future sales. We were encouraged to bring a favorite book to share. I really enjoyed self help books.

After Bela went over the sales goals, she then asked if anyone had a book they would like to share.

"I have a book that I would like to share," I said eagerly. "I am a big fan of self help books. This book is called 'Healthy Selfishness: Getting The Life You Deserve Without the Guilt.' I really like this title a lot because at times I do feel as if I need to be a bit selfish and not to give in too much to everyone's demands or what they want me to do. I would recommend this book to anyone who wants to learn how to change their life and achieve a life of purpose, joy, meaning, and satisfaction."

I enjoyed helping customers, greeting them with a big smile and letting them know I was there to help them. For that part of the job, I had to learn how to order materials on the computer. I had one of my co-workers demonstrate it for me but I knew this could be a problem, given my continued problems with my short-term memory and being able to retain information.

At that moment, I thought about what my dad taught me when I faced situations like these. "Just do your best son and leave the rest to God Almighty," a voice said to me. My father's advice allowed my mind to be at ease and I was very thankful for that.

After the shift was over I apologized to Bella and told her that I would try hard to remember how to order materials by using the stores database.

"Don't worry about it Victor. You know you are doing such a good job, please don't be frustrated. Now go home and relax. Have a good day Victor."

I felt tired and uneasy about what the future would bring. I was still trying to remember the steps of how to order materials and I was fixated on this one task. It would be a new dream to me if I could ever learn how to do this task. I wondered, "Would I ever see it turn into reality."

ALL BECAUSE OF A DRUNK DRIVER! PLEASE DON'T DRINK AND DRIVE

History Repeats Itself

Six years.

For six years, I held the job at the book store, starting at 6 a.m., working until 10, then hustling over to the nursing home where I continued to volunteer.

It was hard, no question, but I got tremendous satisfaction knowing I made a difference. At the bookstore patrons and staff valued my work and efforts I made to go the extra mile. At the nursing home, I worked tirelessly, as if I was getting paid, in the hope someone there would notice and offer me a paid position.

Still, I couldn't help but feel I was headed down the same familiar path where eventually my dreams would be shattered.

At times, my book store supervisor Madge would ask me to work faster. When I told her I was going as fast as possible, she still expected more and more from me. I quietly did my assigned duties and kept silent. It hurt too much to talk about the pain that I felt.

But my real satisfaction came from my work with Mr. A and other residents at the nursing home.

Mr. A and I built a strong friendship, creating memories to last a lifetime. I would take him outside to see the birds and horses, and then go to lunch. After lunch we would watch TV or I would assist him to make calls to his family.

Afterwards I would go to the lower level where I would assist the residents in doing table games, tea parties, poetry reading and other activities. It was a great feeling, seeing their smiles. That was one thing that made volunteering enjoyable for me.

Galations 5:22-23 But the fruit of the spirit is love, joy, kindness, goodness, faithfulness, gentleness, and self control. Against such things there is no law.

For six years this was my schedule as I took care of Mr. A and for three years I assisted with activities work. I did get a bonus once a year during Christmas time and praises all year long of what a great job I was doing. That praise, I hoped, would lead me to a real job in the company but it wasn't to be.

When Mr. A passed away, I left the nursing home. I couldn't afford to volunteer any longer since I needed to pay my bills. I walked away from a place that I had called my home away from home for six years but I did not leave empty handed.

I had received letters of recommendations from Mr. A's daughter who was so grateful for all the care and love I had given to her father for those years, Mr. A's sisters, and Mr. A's nurse who saw my devotion to him.

It was a great feeling to have received so many positive letters. What made me even more joyous was the life that I had touched and how much happier I made his days at The nursing home! I will carry that with me for the rest of my life.

2 Corinthians 9:7 NIV Each man should give what you have decided in your heart to give, not reluctantly or under compulsion, for God loves a cheerful giver.

Now was the time to focus on me and find a job that I would love and appreciate! It did feel strange not having anyone to take care of or anything to do. I thought, "where would I enjoy working?"

I told myself, "I have excellent experience helping people in the nursing home and I have experience in being a companion like I was with Mr A. I also did activity assistant volunteer work as well. I am going to apply at all of the nursing or assisted living homes and pray that they will hire me. That is where my real passion lays. So why not go for it?"

I updated my resume for every position that I would be applying for and went to a few assisted living homes around San Diego County. I was desperate but patient.

After a few months of looking, with no success, I went to a job agency that specialized in finding jobs for disabled people. I felt nervous as I did not know what to expect. I also hated being labeled disabled.

I explained to the agency representative, Tina, I was looking for a job in health care as an activity assistant or companion.

"I have a lot of experience doing this as I was a volunteer for a nursing home," I told her, then handed over my letters of recommendation and resume.

"OK that is good. We'll we will see what we can find. I have a database that I use that sends out notices for any job openings. This may take a few months as this kind of job may be hard to find but we will do it. We will find that job!

"Thank you Tina. This really means a lot to me to have a job working in this field. That is why I volunteered for so long. I wanted to show everyone that I have a passion for this kind of work."

"Yes, I think anyone can clearly see that you do have a passion. These are very good letters of recommendation. I am just going to polish up your resume to make it look a bit better. Your resume is the first thing that the employers will see. Can you go home and type for me a sample cover letter that explains your desire for getting a job in this field and why you want to work in this field? Also keep your eyes open for any places that you would like to apply to. OK I think I may have overwhelmed you with too much work to do?"

"No, it's OK," I replied. "If all this work that we are doing to find a job will lead to success, well then, it is all worth it."

"Oh Victor, I can already feel that you will be getting a job very soon. I love your positive attitude," she said with a big smile.

"Attitude is half the battle. I have a very positive outlook on life. I know I will be a success with the help of God Almighty. He has the perfect job for me."

The help and encouragement I got from Tina was incredibly positive: I was not doing this alone. But it would be a long uphill battle. I couldn't help but wonder if my disability would be a detriment to a future job. My experience with the library haunted me and it remained a puzzle why the nursing home would not hire me after all my volunteer work. All I wanted to do was focus on a bright future A week later, I returned to the job agency and Tina, gave me an updated and improved resume. I gave her a cover letter to a job that I was interested in applying for. It was a job as an activity assistant at a local nursing home.

"Victor this cover letter looks great. Remember for every job that you are going to apply for, you will need a cover letter. Now we are all ready to apply, apply, apply. Your homework assignment from me now is to apply at three different places in the next two weeks. Let's meet back here in two weeks. Are you ready to work? Finding a job is like a job," Tina said to me.

"Well if we work together we will find a job. Thank you for helping me."

"My pleasure. That is why I am here."

"OK then off to work I go."

I wanted to start out with the places of employment that were close to home.

I walked into an assisted living home that was a mile away from my house with my resume in hand and my dress clothes on. I dropped off the resume and filled out the application.

"Can I speak to the activity director and give this to her in person?" I requested of the receptionist.

"I'm sorry sir. She is very busy right now. Don't worry she will get your application and will be in contact with you."

"OK, well thank you so much. I do look forward to hearing from you soon."

Next, I drove to a home-care agency an hour drive from my house. I had to ask myself if this trip was really worth it to drive so far to find employment. When I got there, I had difficulty finding the building. Once there, I walked into the office trying to walk as straight as I could to hide my disability.

"Hi how are you sir, may I help you?" A man in his early thirties said to me.

"I am here to apply for a job."

I was handed an application and it took me about half an hour to fill out, review it, and double check if I had filled out everything correctly.

After I turned it in, he looked over my application, resume, and letters of reference.

"Thank you very much. You do have very good letters of recommendation. We are a home care company, meaning that we do send our employees out to clients' houses.

You will be in charge of doing everything for the client in his/her home. Do you think you will be able to do this kind of work?"

"Yes I will be able to. I have volunteered in a nursing home for six years doing this kind of work for one person," I replied feeling a bit nervous.

"I noticed you walking with a slight limp. Will that affect your performance on the job?"

"Not at all. I can do everything and can take care of people who need assistance."

"OK thank you. I will keep your application on file and we will call you in for an interview very soon."

I walked away from the office with a negative feeling. I did not like the questions I was asked and drove away, trying not to look back on this experience. Was the gas money I spent really worth my trip?

I tried to stay positive after such a long day of searching for a job and e-mailed Tina to tell her how my day went and that I applied for two jobs. Her response: "Good Victor. Let's keep trying. Don't stop until someone hires you and tells you, yes, you are hired."

As I waited for responses from those two places, I prayed that God open the door and show me the way to my dream job.

"Oh heavenly father, God Almighty, I know you have the perfect job waiting for me. I know everything will happen in your timing. I am waiting. I know you can hear me. All my needs, wants, and desires are in your hands. Please LORD show me the way to the job of my dreams. This is all I ask for. Find in those that I applied for a job that they may find me in favor and hire me."

While waiting to hear back, I kept having regular appointments with Tina to see if there were any openings. We met every three weeks as I looked for a job. On this day, she noticed how discouraged I appeared to be. I told her I hadn't heard anything.

"Well, let's keep looking. We must not give up hope," she replied to comfort me.

Romans 12:12 NIV Rejoice in hope, be patient in tribulation, be constant in prayer.

"OK Victor, let's meet again in three weeks and see where we will be at that time. Keep your chin up Victor. Remember we are in this together."

"Thank you Tina. I appreciate that."

In the following weeks, I applied to more home caregivers agencies, some more than an hour away. I was desperate and would go anywhere for a job. My gas money was suffering and I felt like I was blindly rushing into something I could not see. I felt a bit insecure about the path I was on, that it would lead to nowhere.

"Maybe I should just chose another field of work," I said to myself one day. "If no one will hire me in this field, then I have no other option. I feel so heartbroken at times. Is it really my disability that prevents me from getting a job?"

Opportunity Knocks But....

They say God works in mysterious ways. What a cliché, right?

Yet, on one of the darkest days in my continuing search for a job, the light finally started to shine and God brought me to the right place at the right time.

That day I went to another assisted living facility close to my house.

It was the same familiar refrain. I asked for an application for the job I saw on Craigslist, only to be told it had been filled. When I asked to speak to the activity director, I was told she was in a meeting and unavailable.

While I did get her business card, it felt as though I was being pushed out the door and was deliberately kept from meeting the activity director.

I then tried another nursing home, quite a bit away from my house. Again, I was told there were no openings, but I was welcome to fill out an application and return it where they would keep it on file.

As I walked away, I thought something has to come my way. I have been searching for a job near and far to my house. I was so sad, I turned to God. "Oh LORD please help me keep my mind calm. Help me LORD to find a job. I am desperate, driving everywhere, trying to find a place of employment that would want to hire me. LORD only you know the future and what will happen. Let it be bright. Praying that a job come my way. Amen."

That evening, I was so worn out, I went to The YMCA. I needed to sit in the jacuzzi and let my mind escape the travails of the frustrating job search. When I got there, I decided on a nice workout before relaxing in the whirlpool.

As I was working out I met the administrative assistant from the nursing home where I volunteered. Her name was June and she brought her boss, Dakota, to this "Y" to check it out.

"How do you like it here Dakota?" I asked.

"It is good. I am just so used to the other gym I go to. This gym is good as well. How are you doing?"

"I have been doing good. Just trying to find a job in the nursing home."

"Any prospects?"

"No, not yet, but I have just started to look for a job. I will find one soon. God willing."

"Yes well good luck. You will find something soon."

While this conversation was going, I was thinking, "why doesn't Dakota offer me a job?"

I excused myself to burn off some frustration on the Stairmaster and selected my favorite workout, the Fat Burner Plus. I had just started, when June came up and asked if I would be interested in coming in for an interview.

"OK, what position?"

"Caregiver."

"Caregiver?"

"Yes but you will not be doing as much as the other caregivers. You would just stay on the floor and make sure the residents are safe."

"OK I will be there. What time should I come in?"

"11 a.m. would be good. Is that too short notice?"

"No that is perfect. I will be there at 11. See you then."

I was so happy and excited. I happened to be at the gym at the right time when Dakota and June showed up. I quickly finished my workout and went home to tell my mom the good news, how both woman happened to be there at the same time as me.

After congratulating me, my mom reminded me to thank God , that He led you to the YMCA at precisely the right time.

Matthew 19:26 Jesus looked at them and said, "With man this is impossible, but with God all things are possible.

That evening, I prayed that my interview go well and that I get the job.

"Oh LORD father in heaven thank you for bringing me so far in my search for a job. As the sun will rise tomorrow I pray that it be a good day full of opportunities and that everything goes well in this upcoming interview. God thank you for hearing my plea of desperation for a job. If this interview does not go well, then I will keep looking for a job. Father God I know my dad is looking down on me at this time and at all times in my life. Please allow me to live my life in a way that is pleasing to you and my dad. Amen!

Psalm 63:6-7 On my bed I remember you; I think of you through the watches of the night; Because you are my help, I sing in the shadow of your wings.

I arrived promptly at 11 for my interview and was questioned by June and Marshall, the person who had set up my schedule when I was a volunteer. They asked why I was interested in doing this kind of work.

"It is rather a long story but in a nutshell; See, my dad was paralyzed by a drunk driver when I was five years old. He was left in the rehab for 1 year and afterwards was unable to walk for the rest of his life. I was the one who would help him out. We were like a team. I would do such tasks as make him a cup of tea, make his bed, go on outings, pick up his medications, help him to exercise, prepare his meals, and other things. When he passed away I felt very empty inside and wanted to help somebody and that is why I came here to volunteer and help Mr. A until his very last day. I wanted people to see that I have a passion for helping people so that is why I volunteered for so long. I just had to be there for Mr. A as he reminded me of my dad in a lot of ways and when my dad passed away I held his hand and told myself that I will find a job where I can help and inspire people. We all are in the same boat if you think of it."

"I am brain injured, there is no cure, and I am stuck. However I have made it very far in life. I was in a two-month coma and seven month rehab after the car crash that happened when I was five years old. I have come a long way. I would like to be a source of inspiration for these residents. For them to see myself going all the way with my disability will allow them to go all the way with their illness. They will strive to go the extra step just as I have. I think and hope they can see that through me."

"Wow! That was quite a story," Marshall said to me.

"As a caregiver you will be responsible for feeding residents, dealing with dentures, changing their clothes, getting them ready for bed, and taking them to activities. Would you be able to perform all these functions?" June asked.

"I really do not have any experience doing any of these things. I am willing to learn though. I am sure I will be able to do something," I replied nervously.

"What would you do if you saw two residents fighting in the hallway? How would you handle this situation?" Marshall asked.

"I would try to make them to stop fighting. I would separate them from one another and try to make them calm down. If another associate is nearby I can also ask him or her for help."

"What would you do if you observed a resident who was crying and upset? How would you handle this situation?"

"I would comfort the resident by talking to her nicely with words of comfort.

When she has calmed down then I would take her to the TV room or wherever she would like to go and then tell her I will be back in five minutes."

"Can you come back tonight for orientation around 4:00 PM?" Marshall asked.

"I sure can. I am ready. Oh my God I got the job."

"Welcome to the nursing home Mr. Caregiver."

As I walked away, I felt so happy and relieved. I still felt nervous about doing this kind of work. I felt as if I would be in competition with other caregivers. I was just thankful for this opportunity that God gave to me.

All grown up and working at the nursing home
In honor of one of the finest people I know. My dad!

Job Orientation!

Now the job begins.

I came home and told my mom the good news and she congratulated me.

"The Good Almighty LORD sure has blessed you," she said. "Did you say, 'Thank you' to God Almighty?"

"I sure did. I have given thanks to God Almighty about a million times already! I hope all goes well. My first job orientation is tonight. I will get ready. Dad must be very proud of me right now. He is smiling down on me from heaven above. Thank you dad for all your support," I said as I blew a kiss to the sky.

But this was going to be a new experience for me and what scared me the most was the realization I couldn't do everything a caregiver was required to do. That included assistance in the bathroom and help bathing and getting ready for bed. I had no experience in any of those areas...

"Hi Marshall. So where shall I go?" I asked as I arrived that evening.

"OK Mr. Victor. Here is the schedule posted for the day. Looks like you will be up here on the second wing of the building."

I followed Marshall up to the working area and he explained some of my duties.

"We have some that can walk, some that are fall risks and that you will need to keep an eye on. We must also offer the residents snacks when we come in. Here in the cupboard we have crackers, chips, fruit bars etc. We also have bananas, apples, and oranges up here in the fruit bowl on the counter. There is lemonade in the fridge."

"OK," I replied waiting for further instruction.

"That's it for now. I will explain more at dinnertime when all of us take the residents to the dining room," Marshall said to me.

As I interacted with all of the residents, I tried to make them happy. I offered them snacks and lemonade, even told a joke or two. The tricky part to this was surveying the area to make sure no one fell when they walked.

It struck me: I was no longer a volunteer, working one on one like I did with Mr. A. I was now a paid caregiver, with responsibilities to many residents.

When dinnertime came around at 4:30 p.m., the caregivers would transport residents to a huge dining room. I poured drinks, assisted those who needed help eating, and bussed the dishes.

After dinner we would take the residents back to the country kitchen where they would stay until it was time for bed.

It was not my responsibility to assist the residents to go to bed, but to just watch the floor while caregivers were putting them in for the night.

After the orientation, Marshall asked me how I liked the job.

"It is good but I am very nervous and scared."

Marshall patted me on the back and assured me that everything was going to be OK and not be nervous.

I left that night, feeling good about the work I was doing and the positive difference I was making in the lives of the residents at The Nursing Home. I prayed that there would not be any hassles. All I wanted was to be welcomed, accepted, and loved for the work that I would be doing.

As time went by, I got used to the schedule and the daily grind of the day-to day routine, I grew to love my job. I kept my dad in my mind at all times-- he was my focal point and reason I was doing this job. I kept repeating to myself over and over, "I love you dad and I do this work in honor of you."

Every step I took, every person I helped, reminded me of my dad and how I aided him. As I would push a resident down the hall in their wheelchair, I remembered how I did the same for my dad. During dinnertime, while serving residents their drinks and meals I would remember my dad and how I did the same for him. There was just so much good that this job has brought to my life.

I met a resident, by the name of Carter, who I helped and became very fond of. He was able to walk, could feed himself but required a reminder to take a snack before bedtime since he was diabetic. I grew attached to him and he reminded me of my dad in some ways, especially in the way he talked.

Yet, just as I was feeling good and blessed, there was trouble looming I could not detect.

One day, as I entered the kitchen, Kenzie, the manager there, kicked me out because she feared I would fall.

"If you need anything, then please just ask one of us and we will get it for you. Now honey, what did you need?"

"I need a coke for one of the residents," I said feeling sad for myself and my disability. I thought to myself, "I walk just fine. I don't fall down in my kitchen at home." I was very frustrated and thought of my dad and the advice he had given to me.

"My son, be brave as some people may not understand you. We must be very understanding of people and their actions. It may not be fair but life sometimes is not fair when you have a disability. Just walk away son, and don't look back."

As I went back to the country kitchen to watch over the residents, one of the caregivers Abbie asked me, "Victor can you change all of these residents in the bathroom?"

"I was not taught how to do that. I am here to only watch the floor and make sure no one falls down."

"You can not do anything. You can not do anything," she repeated to me as she waved her index finger back and forth at me.

I could not get these two incidents out of my mind. Kenzie kicking me out of the kitchen when I tried to enter and Abbie telling me I could not do anything. I felt I should just go home and forget about this kind of work. It was so heartbreaking. I went to Marshall and explained what was going on and asked how I should handle the situation.

"I cannot work with Abbie anymore or in the section that she works in."

"And why is that?" he responded.

"Because she says that I can not do anything. It's just not nice and I want to leave."

"No Victor. Abbie is the same way with me when I work with her. She is very particular about everything. She is bullying you, which is not nice at all and is against company policies. No one should be treated that way. I want you to go to the administrative assistant and let her know just exactly what is going on.

"Oh Marshall, I can't do that. It hurts to much to talk about it," I responded.

"Well, I can't do anything about this situation but they can. Please go and tell Jean just exactly what is going on here. Please Victor."

"OK I will."

As I went to talk to Jean, I thought about Jesus and how he did not complain about anything. Isn't that why we are here on earth is to live a Christ-like life? I had a feeling that I would be turning the other cheek a lot over here. I was like a boxer in the ring left defenseless as I always believed in turning the other cheek and forgiving my enemies.

Jean asked what I needed.

"I just wanted you to know that Abbie is not being that nice to me and I am very hurt. She keeps telling me very rudely 'you can't do anything, you can't do anything.' She is putting me down every day."

"OK Victor. I will have a talk with her and tell her to stop telling you things like that. Be strong Victor. I will handle this situation."

"I'm sorry Victor," Abbie said to me as I began working my shift. I felt as she sincerely meant it and no one would ever hassle me ever again.

Months later, another problem arose as I was working and a nurse by the name of Cole started to ask me questions about my disability.

"Victor, does it hurt when you walk?"

"A little bit. I handle the pain though so I don't complain."

"Is it hard for you to walk straight?"

"Yes it is. It takes great concentration and effort for me to be able to walk straight. I can take 13 steps straight without limping."

"Can you show me how you can run down the hall and back?"

"No please just leave me alone," I responded with great sadness.

"Does it bother you when I ask you these kind of questions?"

"Yes it does. Can you please stop asking me questions that pertain to my disability?"

"Oh, sorry about that," he apologized and never asked me about my disability ever again.

One night the activity director asked me, "So how do you like your job?"

"I love it," I responded hiding the real answer under my tongue. I often wondered why they did not have me work in activities since it's what I did as a volunteer for so many years. It is a complete mystery to me.

"Victor you know the real reason I would not hire you?" she asked me.

"No, why would you not hire me?"

"Because you are too slow and cannot move fast enough."

I walked away without saying a word feeling even more crushed than before. Now I had the caregiver upstairs telling me that I could not do anything, to the nurse who had asked me questions about my disability, to now the activity director telling me why she would not hire me.

"Oh Jesus please help me. All of these people are torturing me with their words. Please help me God as I want to keep working this job as a caregiver in honor of my dad. I will never let that go. I will do this kind of work forever or as long as you give me the strength to do so."

1 Corinthians 16:13 Be on your guard; stand firm in the faith, be courageous; be strong.

Soon, I started to ask my pastor and the prayer team to pray for me at church every Sunday and I put prayer requests on the church website. The more people that prayed for me and for this very hurtful situation the more support I would receive. I couldn't go through this all alone. Thank God, Jesus was there to comfort me.

Psalm 18:2 The LORD is my rock, my fortress, and my deliverer, my shield and the horn of my salvation, my stronghold.

ALL BECAUSE OF A DRUNK DRIVER! PLEASE DON'T DRINK AND DRIVE!

Crying Tears Of Fear And Pain

Nothing is easy. If anyone knew the meaning of those three words, it had to be me.

I was surprised one day when Dakota, the administrator, asked to talk to me in the nurse's office.

There was no chitchat as she got right to the point.

"Victor, a lot of caregivers are complaining that you are not doing enough work as a caregiver. I don't know where else I can put you. Looks like I will have to let you go as you cannot work for us anymore. Here is your letter of dismissal."

I already had a feeling of where this conversation was going to go.

"I know activities. I volunteered for many years as an activity assistant. I can do that kind of work," I responded.

When she said no to working in activities, my heart sank. I felt used. I felt as if all the hard work I did as a volunteer amounted to nothing.

"Well, what do you want? I am doing all the things that they told me to do in the interview, which is basically to watch the floor and make sure everyone is safe."

I then turned the conversation in a different direction, asking Dakota why she hired me in the first place.

There was no reply for a full minute as Dakota pondered her reply, then said, "Because I thought you would be good to look over the residents while the caregivers put them in bed."

I continued to direct my questions of her.

"Why was I not hired as an activities assistant? I mean I volunteered doing activities work for many years for free. I practically gave up all my desires and needs in life just to help out and prove that I can do this kind of work and now you are telling me that I can't do this kind of work?"

"What do you mean gave up your desires and needs in life?"

"I mean putting everything on hold in my life to be here and help all of these residents. I stopped going to my grievance support group meetings at the hospital to deal with the passing of my father because Mr. A needed me and I felt compassion for him. In the afternoon, I helped out and tirelessly volunteered doing activities work. I did not have to do that but I wanted to. I did all that work so that I could prove to you that I could do this kind of work. Do you mean to tell me that you thought that I did all this work for nothing? I do have proof that I did this work as well."

"What proof do you have?"

"I have all of those activity sheets where my name is written for the activities that I did with the residents."

When she said it didn't mean a thing, I continued to make my case.

"I also have letters of recommendation from a person who has and still works here."

When Dakota asked me who wrote the letter of recommendation, I told her it was a charge nurse named Elly.

When I asked why she wanted to know, she insisted, "Please tell me what she wrote."

"She wrote how good of a volunteer I am and how I helped take care of a resident and did activities work with other residents. She said she would recommend me for activity assistant or to be a care companion. It is a great letter of recommendation."

"Mr. A's sisters and daughter also wrote letters of recommendations for me. His daughter's letter is very nice and explains thoroughly what a great job I did volunteering and taking care of her dad for all those years."

I was on a roll and not willing to let Dakota off the hook.

"I have all that proof to show the judge if we were to go to court. I even have pictures to show proof that I have volunteered here. Either I can leave this place or my lawyer can come in. I don't think you want that to happen, do you?"

Dakota took all this in, then replied deliberately, "Well then, looks like this is a no go."

I had another request, asking Dakota to have her activity director Aleena to leave me alone, explaining she was bothering me.

When she asked for specifics, I tried to maintain my composure, but couldn't. Tears flowed because I never thought I would have to tell this story all over again when the wounds did not, or could ever, heal.

"Do you know that after I had told you that I could not volunteer anymore, a day later she came to me and told me that I must continue to volunteer for her. Now she keeps telling me reasons why she did not hire me as activity assistant saying that I can not move fast enough."

"One time she laughed at me because I could not walk as fast as she could. She has done no good to me but has just hurt me. Do you know Dakota, at one point I did want to talk to your boss? I didn't though. I forgave you."

"If you would have talked to my boss I would have been fired. I would have had to look for another job."

"Yeah, I can forgive you but here you are ready to fire me," I said sadly.

"No Victor, don't worry I am not going to fire you. I was unaware of the situation. I will talk to Aleena and let her know about the discussion that we just now had," she said as she angrily scrunched up the letter of resignation that she was going to give to me and threw it in the trashcan.

As I left, Dakota kept staring at me as I went back to the country kitchen to help the residents.

"Cindy how are you doing today?" I asked a resident, and handed her a glass of water.

As she drank the water I thanked God Almighty for giving me the strength to speak up. If I hadn't I probably would have been let go, just like at the library. I felt like a cornered boxer, just trying to defend myself. I kept telling myself is that I would NOT be knocked out; instead I would try to stand strong with the help of God Almighty!

> **Isaiah 12:2 Surely God is my salvation; I will trust and not be afraid.**
> **The LORD, the LORD, is my strength and defense; he has become my salvation.**

ALL BECAUSE OF A DRUNK DRIVER! PLEASE DON'T DRINK AND DRIVE

LORD I'm Calling Out Mercy

I had hoped all along to find my place.

The nursing home operated throughout San Diego. I had worked in three of the neighborhoods, and in each one, I felt unwanted and unappreciated. Many times, other caregivers would denigrate me saying I wasn't a true caregiver. I felt truly sad and unwanted.

Then, I was assigned the East neighborhood, I prayed that God help me stay in this job; I do this work in honor of my dad. Please God Almighty, allow that honor to live on, and enable me to be there for these people as I was there for my dad.

When I checked in, I was welcomed as an equal and as I began working , these co-workers let me help in ways where in other neighborhoods, I was limited in what I could do.

I was allowed to take a few residents to activities, and even put a few to bed. It made me feel wanted and appreciated. I even met a resident, Landon, who reminded me a lot about my father.

"So how are you doing Victor?"

"I am doing good. I am happy to be here helping you."

"I am very happy to have you help me too. Can you put my toothbrush and toothpaste on my sink so I can brush my teeth?"

"Yes right away. I will do that," I replied feeling a sense of happiness that I was making a positive difference.

Helping him took me back as I recalled how I assisted my dad in the same way. Sometimes Landon would want some fruit before bedtime so I would take him to the kitchen to have an orange and a banana.

My dad was the same; he would always eat two servings of fruit everyday. Sometimes I

would sit with Landon in the TV room and we would watch a classic film. He enjoys pictures from back in the day such as "Some Like It Hot" with Tony Curtis and Jack Lemon, or Doris Day movies. Every time we were together, I thought of my dad and remembered how we watched TV together.

I would also help other residents get ready for bed, aiding them with their bed clothes, and brushing their teeth. Yes, it is my honor to help and take care of them in the same fashion I helped my dad. I don't think of my job as work; I look at it as another day helping others as I remember my dad. My dad's honor will live on forever and ever.

Sometimes I think it is all too good to be true, to be this happy, doing what I love in honor of my dad, but I am forever grateful to God Almighty for helping me to see the light at the end of every dark tunnel and to bring smiles to everyone's face.

Psalm 40:1-3
After all the waiting and all the patience and all the trusting I think I can handle it's good to know I can see the light at the end of the tunnel... he set my feet on a rock and gave me a firm place to stand.

Some Things That Seem Too Good To Be True Just Might Be

I was flourishing, loving every moment of my job. It was as if God had blessed me beyond what I could have ever dreamed or deserved.

The charge nurse and caregivers had assigned me to three residents. I took them to their chosen activity, served them dinner and helped them at bedtime. I aided other caregivers by lifting and transferring residents.

I especially enjoyed my time with Landon who reminded me of my dad as I helped him change his shirt, get his toothbrush ready, assist with toileting and finally be put to bed. It was something that I loved and looked forward to doing.

Many times, he'd request a snack, vanilla pudding, the same as my dad.

Next, I would help Hadley, a very sweet woman who was very easy to take care of since she had no trouble walking. I provided the same care that I gave Landon. In addition, I took off her glasses, and removed her dentures before going to bed and put them in a safe place.

My third resident's name was Cale, a gentleman with a very thick southern accent. As with Landon and Hadley, he required the same care but needed to be lifted up. Once up, he could stand on his own. It was a great honor to be doing this kind of work.

"I hope this would never end and that I will be able to do this for a long time," I said to myself every evening at work. "Could this all be too good to be true?"

A while later the bomb dropped. It were like the devil stepping into my territory and preventing me from enjoying the work that I was doing.

On that night, as I was assisting Landon in the restroom, I heard a fellow co-worker talking to the nurse about how dangerous it was for me to be doing this kind of work. The charge nurse, Jackie, came into the restroom where I was assisting Landon and asked me to step outside for a minute.

"Victor, I do not want you to assist any residents that you have to lift. If you want to continue to help Landon, then you can only do the brushing and the changing of his shirt. Someone else will provide all other care. Do you understand me?" she said sternly.

"Yes," I responded but my heart and soul sank. It was a mystery why my responsibilities, and the people I was taking care of were reduced. I had not injured any of the residents in my care. It just did not make sense.

A week later the department of health services calls me into the office.

"Hi Victor, how are you?" Alexa asked me.

"Good," I responded.

"Victor are you helping residents in the restroom and helping them to get ready for bed?"

"Yes, but I stopped helping them since the nurse told me not to, " I responded.

"Victor I do not expect you to assist residents in that way. You are to be more like a companion for the residents. Talk to and engage with them in that way," she responded.

"Yes but I still can take care of Hadley since she can walk," I said, fighting for my rights.

"But she fell down the other day as one person in the activities department was helping her."

"Don't worry, if she in my care, she will not fall down. I can promise you of that."

"OK then but we must be very careful then that she does not fall down," Alexa responded.

I thought, why is she saying these things to me? It was driving me crazy, another puzzle I could not solve.

I continued to work and I know there was a reason why I was led to this place.

I care for Hadley with a full heart just like I did for Landon, Cale, and most importantly, my dad, who looks down on me from heaven and I know is proud of me.

My shift is 2:30-11:00 p.m. and every night when I put Hadley to bed and leave for the night, I feel good about all my efforts. I even see many stars shining down on me when I walk out the door but one particular star catches my eye and I know my dad is winking down to me. Many times there would be a half moon and I can envision my dad looking and checking up on me as he is smiling at all of the work that I do in honor of him.

"Thank you dad for shining your light on me and for the love you gave to me," I say as I blow a kiss to the sky!

My Dad's Advice

Ever since the crash, I felt God was my only shield from the hurtful words people would direct to me.

While I could count on my family for support, there was also God Almighty to hear my prayers and give me practical advice. I heard stories from the bible from my dad who reminded me constantly God would always be there for me. He and I had discussions about life.

"Have courage my son and be brave in all the storms of life. You and I have learned this the hard way. Whenever you face difficulty in life, always remember that God is there for you. I will not be here someday but God, our eternal father is always there for us, forever and ever. Remember the life that Jesus had on the cross and how he forgave his enemies.

Matthew 5:43-45 You have heard the law that says, "Love your neighbor and hate your enemy. But I say love your enemies! Pray for those who persecute you! In that way, you will be acting as true children of your Father in heaven. For he gives his sunlight to both the evil and the good, and he send rain on the just and unjust alike.

"That law is too hard for me to obey dad," I replied.

"The ways of the LORD are hard, my son, but they are the only way to peace in your heart. We must learn how to forgive and walk away."

"Yes dad, but, but," I replied but immediately interrupted.

"There are no buts Victor. You must remember my words in your life. God is your only shield from the enemy or from those who hurt you. People are only there for you temporarily but God is there for you forever."

"But dad, should I let people trample all over me, when they say such hurtful words to me or make fun of me when they imitate the way I walk or talk."

"In cases like that, remember to walk away from those people. After you have walked away, pray for them. Pray they be nice to you and other people in the future. Remember we can only control our own actions and not other people in what they do."

"OK dad I will try," I replied

"OK Son, thank you. Trust me, it is the only way to live. Can you make one promise to me son?"

"OK, what is it?"

"That you will never turn to drugs for an easy escape to your problems. Drugs are so harmful. The person who hit us and caused this car crash that all of us suffered in was high on drugs and alcohol. Do not turn to anything that will harm you. Such things as throwing your money around, and trying to please people is not good. Only depend on God Almighty for support."

"I will promise you that I will never take drugs and I will always depend on God Almighty.

Where there is an impact to be made I am on my way!

Spoke at this event! Disability

Appeared on Fox 5 News twice

Annual Safety 5k event!

Collaborating with other people to put the alcohol and drug problem to an end!

Speak to many DUI offenders every month at the courthouse

The Agenda for the meeting!

Thanks from Teen Driving Safety 5k Team!

Thank you Ian for allowing me to impact the many people at your event every year!

Epilogue: Faith In Action

Romans 8:28 And we know that God causes everything to work together for the good of those who love God and are called according to his purpose for them.

God has brought me through some very turbulent times. I thank God Almighty everyday and believe God has a purpose or a calling for everyone's life.

My calling, has been to spread my message to NOT drink and drive. I struggled to come to this conclusion but it is what I feel. I do not want anyone to feel the same pain and struggles that I have endured and still am dealing with today. All of us need to live healthy, prosperous lives.

These days, I look for opportunities to speak against driving under the influence. I go to the local court house and give talks to DUI offenders to tell my story. I also have appeared on the news outlets, given talks in schools, and to various organizations.

I see reports about car crashes involving a driver under the influence way too often and that means another person whose life has been turned upside down. It all needs to end.

I have faith in God Almighty that someday there will be zero DUI offenders and our streets will be safe. That is my dream. I have a saying: "Please don't drink and drive as we all need to survive and live healthy lives; no one can have a life like mine."

It takes a lot of courage to speak in public and relate my life story. Sometimes I just want to keep mum and just not say anything, but then think, "if I don't say anything the situation would just get worse."

It took me one year of listening to the other victims speak about how their lives were affected by a drunk driver at Mothers Against Drunk Driving (MADD) meetings before I could tell the story of the horrible crash that turned my family's life upside down.

I remember being so nervous the first time, trying to catch my breath and shaking in fear, but I made it though. Only God Almighty can do that and He's been there for every uphill battle and downhill dive.

If saving lives is your dream, let's make it a reality. Stop this craziness. It would shatter my heart if I saw any more of my family members or friends killed or injured by a drunk driver. That's why I am writing this book, to prevent this from happening again.

I used to say, "I was involved in a drunk driving accident. That's why I walk with a limp and have limited use of the left side of my body." Now, I replace he word

"accident" with "crash" because drinking or using drugs while driving is no accident. All of these terrible crashes could have, and can be prevented if people make the choice to, put down their keys before they end up throwing away the keys to someone else's future dreams.

My life, along with my late father's, has not been easy. I still to this day have trouble walking, talking, and using the left side of my body. I am sometimes still called retard when someone walks past me. People sometimes ask me why my left hand keeps hitting my rear end. It's very hard for me to keep up with college-level classes since my short term memory remains slightly affected. To pass one class it takes me 9-10 hours of studying just to get a passing grade. How am I supposed to earn a bachelors, masters or obtain a higher level of education? It is literally imposable. All of these problems from one drunk driver.

My mission in life is to prevent anyone from going through what I have gone through! I thank Jesus for the opportunities that he afforded me, and the chance he has given me to spread my message. I hope you will help me to complete my mission by taking a stand and saying no to driving under the influence.

Thank you and God Bless.

Victor S. Grewal

Roller Coaster-The Scariest Roller Coaster Ride 1 Drunk Driver Put 1 Family Through and How Jesus was their only light.

Made in the USA
San Bernardino, CA
02 May 2018